Zero Cost

Self Publishing

How to Self-Publish your book, market internationally, and not spend a cent

2nd Edition

by

Stephen C Norton

A Northwind Ink Publication

Published by Stephen Norton at NorthwindInk

ISBN: 978-1-927343-31-9 Softcover
ISBN: 978-1-927343-32-6 .EPUB format
ISBN: 978-1-927343-33-3 .mobi format
ISBN: 978-1-927343-34-0 .pdf format

Other Editions Available
This book is available in other formats at
www.StephenCNorton.com

as always

For Gail

Books by the Author

Non-Fiction

Breaking Glass - Stained Glass Art and Design
> An introduction to creating stained glass art, including tools, safety, materials, design, techniques and assembly.

Shaping Stone Vol I - The Art of Soapstone Carving
> An introduction to the art of soapstone carving, including tools, safety, materials, design, techniques and finishing.

Shaping Stone Vol II - Advanced Techniques of Soapstone Carving
> Volume II picks up where Volume I ended, guiding you easily and seamlessly into the advanced tools and techniques of soapstone carving.

Zero Cost Self Publishing
> A guide on how to self publish your book, in paper and eBook formats, market internationally, collect royalties and do it all at no cost.

Fiction

The Marseille Scrolls
> The First Jeanne-Marie DeNord Suspense Novel
> 1st century scrolls found in 2009 in Southern France leave Jeanne-Marie in a cat and mouse game with unknown adversaries, as she hunts for answers. If she doesn't find them soon, the scrolls will be buried for another 2,000 years, and maybe Jeanne along with them.

The Exodus Scrolls
> The Second Jeanne-Marie DeNord Suspense Novel
> Jeanne finds herself in the middle of a disaster in Egypt, re-enacting the Exodus plagues. Now Jeanne is in a race to find the answer before the tenth plague kills her and half the world.

A Tapestry of Words and Demons
> A book of poetry, thoughts, images and demons, from the early years.

Songs of Words and Demons
> A book of poetry, thoughts, images and demons, from the middle years.

Demon Dreams
> A compilation of poetry.

Available in paperback and eBook formats.

www.StephenCNorton.com

About the Author

Stephen started his career as a marine biologist, later switched to managing computer support and development teams and is now a full time author, artist and publisher. He lives on the West Coast of Canada with his wife and two crazy cats. An artist for most of his life, he's worked in many mediums, from oil painting to blown glass. For the last 15 years he's focused on writing, publishing, carving soapstone sculptures and creating stained glass art.

He has nine books currently available in both paperback and eBook formats, including two novel, 'how-to' books on self publishing, soapstone carving and stained glass art and three poetry books. He has at least five more books planned for the next few years.

Stephen can be contacted via his personal web site, which also provides links to all sites selling his books, including CreateSpace, Amazon, Smashwords, Barnes & Noble, Apple iTunes, Kobo, Sony and other resellers, at:

www.StephenCNorton.com

Stephen is the founder and CEO of his own publishing company, Northwind Ink, which specializes in publishing and distributing soft-cover and eBooks for new authors. All his books have been self-published using the techniques described in this book. Books published by Northwind Ink include novels, memoirs, 'how-to' books and poetry. Northwind Ink's services are available at:

www.NorthwindInk.com

Disclaimer

Contents

Introduction

The world of publishing has changed dramatically in the last five to ten years. In the past, publishing companies had to believe in a new author enough to risk tens of thousands of dollars in publishing and promoting them. If the new author worked out, the publishing company stood to make a lot more money, but if the new author didn't work out that investment was lost. Being the first to publish a new author's first book was, and still is, a high risk proposition.

While those companies still exist, the smaller window for success in today's fast moving environment means that the risks are even higher. The risk of publishing a new author today is much higher than it was five or ten years ago, and the potential for loss to the publishing company is a lot higher too. Sales of paper books, both hardcover and softcover, have been slowly declining over the past 10 years as eBooks start to make their presence felt. Initially eBooks were a very small part the market but over time their market share has grown. The advent of tablets, eBook readers, and especially smart phones with good quality screen an eBook reader software on board, have suddenly made eBooks much more attractive to the general public. It's now possible to store dozens of eBooks on your phone and read them on your way to work, or on that ten hour plane flight. Some adverts aimed at people going away for a period of time, compare carrying a stack of six or ten paperbacks to the equivalent of loading twenty or thirty eBooks onto their phone or tablet. The comparison is obvious, and the eBooks always win.

EBooks are indeed a way of the future, though lately they seem to have reached a plateau of about 30% of the market. I doubt paper books will ever disappear. There's just something so physically satisfying about holding a book in your hands and turning paper pages. However the success of eBooks has introduced new companies into the publishing environment. Companies that are there specifically to create and distribute eBooks and a new approach to publishing has developed. The Internet has also supported the new companies as they're much easier and more productive for the new author to work with.

These new companies are there specifically to help you, the author, succeed, because if you succeed, they make money. Sounds a bit odd, doesn't it? You're working so they can make money, but think it through. For them to make money the books have to sell. If the books sell then you must be making money too.

In the traditional publishing world, if you are successful, you would make five, possibly ten percent of the cover price, while the publishing house took the other ninety percent. In the new publishing environment it's almost the reverse. You can make anywhere from thirty to seventy-five percent of the cover price, while the publisher / distributor takes the remainder. That means that by helping them make money, you are receiving a much larger share of the pie. In my business career, the term 'a Win:Win solution' was very popular. It seldom worked that way, because most business relationships tend towards having a winner and a loser. However, in the new publishing environment, I do believe we are dealing with a Win:Win proposition.

The other factor that comes into play, especially important for new authors, is that under the old publishing environment, it was, and still is, very difficult for a new author to break into the market. To succeed in the traditional paradigm, the new author first has to win the interest of an agent, who must then catch the interest of a publishing house. Given the current economic climate and the decreasing sales potential for paper based books, it's very hard for new authors to break through.

In the new publishing environment, the on-line publishing companies provide the tools to enable the new author to basically publish themselves. The second key factor that these companies provide, in addition to the publishing tools, is distribution to truly global markets.

If you do a Google search for 'self publishing companies' you'll get eleven million and more responses. Now scan through those websites and see what they offer. They all have two things in common. First they all claim to provide publishing and distribution services to order. Some say it's free but when you get down to the fine print all of these services have a fee attached. They all want the author to pay a fee to be published and they all suggest (strongly) that the cost will be recovered from the author's royalty payments at some time in the future. I don't buy that line.

Over the course of several years of searching though, I have found and now use three organizations that really do offer free self-publishing for the author. That means free from start to finish, no hidden extras, no extra fees, no completion costs, free! These three companies really do offer zero cost self-publishing, including international distribution and they do pay royalties.

In order for any author to take part in the new publishing environment, they need to learn which companies will work with them, what tools are available and how to make the best use of those tools. In this book I will introduce you to those three companies and I'll show you how you really can get your book published, in both paper and multiple eBook formats, distribute and sell to real global markets and pay no up front or ongoing costs. Your books will have an excellent chance of being sold and when they do you will get royalty payments.

These companies provide the tools, support and distribution you need to succeed. I'll show you the tools that are available and teach you how to use them. I'll also give you an idea of how much technical ability you'll need to complete each step. Some steps are a little complex, but don't worry. If you can use a computer, you can publish your book.

After describing the tools I'll show you how to access the mechanisms that provide global distribution of your books via all the major web based sales networks, including Amazon, Apple iTunes, Barnes and Noble, Kobo, Sony and others. Best of all, the three companies I'll introduce you to will let you do all this, **at absolutely no cost to you.** When your book sells they will all pay you anywhere from thirty to seventy-five percent royalties, based on your cover price.

For no more than the cost of this book, I can show you how to get that first book published, distributed and selling internationally. And it doesn't stop at the first book. You can repeat the process for as many books as you can produce, all for free. Once you know the basics, the world will open up for you.

Join me, and let's start the journey to becoming a published, internationally selling author, today, at no risk and zero cost!

Why Do I Write?

I've been writing since I was a kid. English composition was my favorite subject in high school. My favorite books were all science fiction, so most of what I wrote was science fiction too. I always thought I would write a science fiction book at some point in my life. Thirty years later I wrote and published my first book, which, surprisingly, had nothing to do with science fiction. It was a mystery / suspense called **'The Marseille Scrolls'**, and combined modern day archaeology with first century scrolls and manuscripts containing a secret.

I write because I enjoy writing, and I've found that the more I write, the more subjects and topics occur to me to write about.

I have read many books on how to write and what to write. Usually they recommend you find a marketplace that will pay you or that you think you can make money in, select a subject within that market and write about that subject. Initially, I found that to be distasteful. One good paying marketplace is romance fiction and I read the book to mean I should be writing romance fiction because that's where the money was. That annoyed me because I had no interest at all in writing romance fiction.

However, after completing my first novel, while I was going through the pain and agony of wasting my time trying to find an agent, I was also pursuing my artistic endeavors, carving soapstone and creating stained-glass art, which I sell in the local galleries. By chance I came across that same book again, telling me to write a book about a subject which would make money rather than a subject which I would enjoy. I realized I might have misunderstood the intent and immediately began work on my first 'how-to' book **'Shaping Stone - an introduction to the art of carving soapstone'**.

Because I enjoyed carving soapstone, creating the book was also enjoyable.

So the moral of this little tale is to definitely read the books on what to write. You don't have to do what they tell you, but they can certainly give you ideas. I've since written several more books and I have several more books underway, in a wide variety of subject areas and topics. Maybe one day I'll even get around to writing my science fiction stories.

One thing I have found, which had never occurred to me when I was contemplating science fiction as a kid, is that writing a book of almost any type requires some fairly detailed and in-depth research. You can't just make things up as you go along, because the reader will usually recognize that and it will detract from the quality of the book. If you're going to write historical fiction you should know that historical period fairly well. From my own reading I've long known if you're going to write high quality science fiction, you need a good understanding of the science that you're writing about. People will no longer accept a faster than light starship drive without some level of technical explanation based to some extent on current science. Star Trek and other space movies have made writing science fiction much more difficult, as the average reader now knows all about warp drives, worm holes and dark matter. I'm quite sure it was much easier writing science fiction in the forties and fifties because anything could be made to sound plausible. So, do your research well, because poor research will make for a poor book.

So, conclusions in short form:

- write because you enjoy writing
- write about things you enjoy writing about
- do enough research to keep the storyline plausible, don't make things up without providing some support
- jot down storylines as they occur to you. You may not use them for years, if ever, but they may be your next great novel.

How to Write

With a chapter heading like that how can I resist. I'm not going to tell you how to write!

While I admit I have read a number of books on how to write I've always found them to be a bit presumptuous. Especially because the books on how to write are not usually written by well-known, successful, best-selling authors. If you check a few best sellers, you'll also find that many of them break 'the rules'.

So instead of telling you how to write, I'll tell you how I write. First I come up with an idea, which can come from anywhere, at any time. Scribble down the basic idea before you lose it. I'll then jot down a rough outline of what I think the book is going to look like, or maybe even a table of contents, chapter headings and such. I may even write some chapters, but they may not, and probably are not, in any particular order. I don't tend to write novels sequentially, starting at the beginning and writing until I hit the end. More often than not I write all over the place. It's not uncommon for me to wake up at three o'clock in the morning with an entire scene crammed in my head and madly scribble down what's in my brain. Hopefully the next morning I can decipher my handwriting. Whatever you do, don't tell yourself that you'll remember that idea because it's so great, roll over and go back to sleep. Come morning, you'll remember you had a great idea, but you'll have absolutely no idea what it was. Get up and write down the idea when it occurs to you!

I've also found that the way I write rather depends on the book I'm writing. My first novel was written in non-sequential pieces, many of them in the middle of the night. Other chapters were written because I had a thought that I wanted to get down and the thought turned into more than just a few notes. I simply wrote until I ran out of that particular scene.

My 'how-to' books are written in a completely different manner.

Because my how-to books cover a project from beginning to end, the subject sequence is built-in. When I wrote **Shaping Stone**, I started with the tools, covered safety, and then began at the raw stone block. The process was quite different from writing my novel because I was taking pictures and videos all along the way, and they became an integral part of the book. Usually I would carve a bit, photograph, and take videos. Then I'd embed the photographs in a Word document, in the correct sequence, and then write directly around the photographs. Wherever I realized I'd missed something, I'd write that section, then go back to carving the stone and taking the missing photographs. On a book like that it's important to take pictures of every step, because once the stone is cut, it's very difficult go back and take pictures of the stone before it was cut.

Several of the books I've read on how to write recommend defining the entire structure of the book: the plot, the sequence, the beginning and the end. They recommend not only identifying the characters, but also detailing them out so that you really get to know them. I found that to be far too formal and artificial, and the resulting works felt very artificial and flat. Too much attention to minute details up front forced the book into too rigid a pathway. To my way of thinking that defeats the entire purpose of writing, and turns the enjoyment into 'work'.

I found that as I wrote, using my 'all over the place' approach, the characters tended to take on a life of their own and grow in unexpected and sometimes very surprising directions as the book progressed. **The Marseille Scrolls** started with a hero, but a third of the way through 'he' morphed into a 'she', because a heroine made the plot line hang together so much better and the storyline took on a much more interesting flow. At one point I needed the heroine to remember a dramatic moment in her life, so I added a brother, whom I immediately killed off. If I had followed the recommended guideline of creating my characters in detail before I started, I would have been constrained to make my storyline work around my predefined character sets. Life isn't like that. I found in many cases the heroine or hero had to be adjusted to meet the storyline as it developed.

Having said that though, I've also found that the storylines themselves change as you go along, and allowing them to change and find their own pathways seems to produce a much better end result, at least for me. I will admit that writing the way I do, with chapters written out of sequence as they occur to me, is a bit more chaotic and requires a bit more work at the end, figuring out how the chapters should sequence properly. It may require more work and patience than following a predefined structure, but I find it much more enjoyable because I discover new things as I go along. My story and my characters are creating and developing themselves, and to some extent me as well, as the story progresses.

So, my recommendations. By all means read the books on how to write. Play around with the different styles, methods and processes they suggest and find the style and process which works for you. There's no need to slavishly follow the recommendations of a book, not even this one. Write in any way that you find works for you. Even then, you may find that a style you've developed for one genre of book doesn't work very well for another genre. As I've mentioned, my novel writing style is quite different from my 'how-to' writing style, so I use them both, as appropriate. Don't try and force yourself into a framework some book recommends as the 'best way to write'. The best way to write is the way you enjoy and the way you produce the best work you can.

So, conclusions in short form:

- write in the manner that best suits you and allows you to produce the best book you can

- read the books on how to write, but adapt their recommendations to fit your own style

- there are no rules, only guidelines and recommendations

Being the Writer

The classic image of the author is that of a slightly scruffy young man in a seedy little apartment, the 'garret', earnestly pounding away on a typewriter. Sadly that never worked for me as my typewriter typing speed was something in the order of only five or ten words per minute.

The updated image is pretty much the same picture except now he or she is pounding away on the keyboard of a laptop or a desktop computer. My keyboard speed is slightly better than my typewriter speed, but not by much.

How you get the words from your brain into the computer so they can be published on paper is a key part of how you write. My preferred writing method was, and still is for the most part, pen and paper, writing longhand. With a pen, my handwriting can almost keep up with my thoughts as I develop a scene. Once I run out of writing, I then transposed the creation into my word processor via the keyboard. Back to old-fashioned typing.

I got pretty tired of that game while writing my first 80,000 word book and started looking for a better solution. I tried laptops and tablets, hoping to capture and convert my handwriting as I went, substituting the tablet screen for the paper, but repeated trials with various software suggested that that was not particularly useful. The tablet and laptop programs can capture block writing reasonably well, 'a b c d', but fail miserably when it comes to recognizing handwritten *'script'*, using connected letters, especially when I'm writing quickly. When I'm trying to keep up with my thoughts, my handwriting often degrades to the equivalent of a doctors scribble on your prescription, so 'so-so' script transcription software simply isn't a workable solution.

From trying to capture handwriting I moved on to trying to capture speech. Windows and Word 2003, and I expect Apple too, come with a default audio capture software tool, which is surprisingly good for free software, but is probably only eighty-five to ninety percent accurate. That means that for every hundred words you speak, you can expect to get ten to fifteen incorrect words. That may not sound bad, but it gets pretty annoying, pretty quickly. Embedded in your document, the erroneous words can often make the entire sentence meaningless and you're left trying to figure out exactly what it was you were trying to say.

I decided to go with the slightly more extravagant route and bought the home version of Dragon Naturally Speaking, a software package for my Windows desktop computer, which, after a bit of training, has an accuracy of ninety-eight to ninety-nine percent. One or two errors per hundred words seems fairly reasonable to me. The program also allows you to add your own words to the recognition dictionary and you can continue to train it to your voice as much as you want.

So for my next few books I wrote longhand, then dictated them back into Word on my computer. For many, many years I used WordPerfect, but the rest of the world has gone Word, so I finally gave up the fight and converted. I haven't tried OpenOffice or StarOffice as I have no idea how well their 'Save as Word' options will work when I submit my finished document to the conversion programs used by the various publishers. However, staying within the 'zero cost' mandate of this book, if you don't own Word already, give OpenOffice or StarOffice a try. Just remember to save your document in Word 2003 format.

Dragon Naturally Speaking allows me to read my handwritten draft aloud into a microphone and Dragon converts it into usable text in Word. Where I used to type a page every ten or fifteen minutes, I can now dictate an entire chapter every ten or fifteen minutes. A huge savings of time and effort and it's definitely much less of a pain in the wrist than the old way. I have tried dictating text directly, and I'm doing that now for much of this book, but I still find for novels and story lines it's better for me to handwrite them than to try dictating directly. Dictating often lags behind my speaking speed and I have to pause every now and again to ensure all my words were properly captured, thus breaking the train of thought. If I don't pause and check, that one wrong word in a hundred can still leave me wondering what I was actually trying to say.

On the flip side, if I feel creative during the day, I am starting, albeit slowly, to dictate directly into Word via Dragon, omitting the handwriting stage entirely. The more I dictate directly, the more comfortable I become with the process, and the more and more I use it. But I haven't got there completely yet. I still handwrite a great deal, especially when I get struck with inspiration at 3 AM.

In any case, there is no real right or wrong way to get your thoughts into your word processor. Some people dictate into a tape recorder and then have someone transcribe it. If you type well, and can type as fast as you can compose in your head, then go direct and emulate the traditional image of the writer. Hopefully I will soon get to a point where I can Dragon Speak everything. Who knows?

It's all a matter of personal choice. Find something that works for you and use that process. Write using whichever method you find to be the most comfortable and productive. Under the 'zero cost' mandate, typing or using the free word recognition software works. Dragon is not a required item.

One word of caution when writing. Don't worry about your word processor setup. For now you can ignore things like page setup, widths, styles, fonts, etc. At this point all we care about is getting the text into the word processor. Formatting, styles and fonts will all come later when we begin the publishing setup process. Just one codicil to that statement. If you plan on producing epub format eBooks, which is strongly recommended, don't use tabs or multiple spaces for spacing as the converter will reject them. Use of Word's 'Increase Indent' tool does pretty much the same thing as tabs and is accepted. The converter also rejects Word's tables, so if you use them in the paper version be prepared to replace them before creating the eBook version.

The other exception is photographs and pictures. In order for photographs to reproduce cleanly in printed books, the original in your document really should be a high quality image. To get that print-ready image quality does take some work. We'll cover the details of how to prepare your images in a later chapter, but make sure you read that chapter before you start embedding images of any kind in your document. A low quality image (low dot-per-inch or dpi), when printed in your book, will look very pixelated, granular and the color will be poor, often really ugly. Presenting a poor quality picture in the middle of your book will ruin the readers impression of your book, so make sure the pictures are of the highest possible quality.

When I write, especially at 3 AM, I tend to write a scene or possibly a chapter. This scene may, but probably isn't, in sequence with the rest of the book. In fact it's not unusual for me to write an early chapter one night, a late chapter the next, and a middle chapter a week later. Because of this rather odd approach to writing, I've found it's best to make each scene or chapter a separate word document. Then at some point, usually when I've got half to three quarters of the book written, I'll rename the files to put them in the sequence I think works best. For example I use filenames like '10 learning in Alexandria', '20 betrayal in Kentucky', '200 farewell to it all'. I leave lots of numbers in between so I can add files or renumber them easily. Once the files are sequenced to the way I think they should be, I create a single master document and import each chapter file into it. The import process is simple.

Open a new blank master document. Open a chapter. Use Word's 'Select all' function to ensure you grab everything in the chapter file. Then copy everything selected (I use CTRL C), click the mouse cursor into the destination location in the master document and then paste what you've copied (I use CTRL V). Close the chapter file and go on to the next chapter file. Continue until all the chapter files have been imported into the master in the same chapter sequence you named them. Then create a new folder called 'original chapters' or something equally creative, and move all the single chapter files into that folder. From now on you will work only on the master file.

For backup and recovery purposes, I create a new copy of the master file whenever I make changes. Name the master something like 'Master April 15, 2013'. Next time you make edits, make a copy of 'Master April 15, 2013' and immediately move the copy into a folder called 'backup copies'. Rename the master and update the date to 'Master April 20, 2013'. You now have two files, with dates built in to the file names, one of which is in a backup folder. The latest date is the most recently edited version of your document. That way, if disaster strikes during an edit, you can go back to yesterdays version of your master document and minimize what you've lost. I also copy the older files onto a second physical drive once a week or so, just in case my entire computer fails. The second drive can be inside your computer, if you have two drives in your machine, or an external plug-in USB or FireWire device, or even onto a large USB plug. Just so you have a second copy on a different physical device from your computer. Backups are useless clutter, until you really need one, then they're priceless.

So, we've covered

- writing styles and processes
- dictation tools
- issues around pictures and photos
- file management and backup.

Technical Complexity: low

Should have familiarity with a word processor, preferably MS Word, and file management on computers.

Items Required for Publishing

Let's switch gears a bit and look at some of the pieces we'll need for publishing the book.

Obviously you need your document, but probably the most important thing the author requires when publishing the book is something people very rarely think about. That is, the author must have sole and uncontested ownership of everything that he or she publishes in their book. You are allowed to quote other people's books providing the quote is short and properly referenced. If you use photographs in your book you must either own the original photograph or have purchased it from the person who took the photograph and have written authorization from the original owner. If you're creating an audio CD which has music playing in the background, you must have the rights to use that background music or you must have created the music yourself from scratch and therefore you own it. Much of the information presented on the web is by definition 'public' but even that can cause some issues.

We will use three companies for publishing our book, CreateSpace, Amazon and Smashwords. I intend to make use of computer screen shots of the various stages of the processes, as a step-by-step guide for the reader, as we walk through the publication process of each company. All of the web screen shots are from publically accessible web sites, however, that doesn't mean you shouldn't request the right to use them. Any web site, and especially those which display a copyrighted symbol or trademark should be considered to be copyrighted and thus you require permission to use them. Happily in this case, Smashwords, CreateSpace and Amazon all gave me permission to use screen shots from their sites. Please bear in mind though, that these are screen shots of active, in-production web sites, and thus subject to change at any time. All three companies update their web sites as and when required, usually to add new features, so please keep in mind that what you see in this book and what you see when you go to the sites may not be exactly the same. Having said that, the screens should be similar enough that you will be able to follow along.

As demonstrated by this issue, it's very important to clarify any copyright issues before you attempt to publish your book. Just because something is freely available to you does not mean you can make use of it in your book. All three sites have a statement that you must agree to prior to publishing, which basically says you have ownership of or right-to-use for all contents published in your book. Publicly accessible or public domain is not the same as you having ownership. If you don't own everything in your book, you must re-assess what you're doing. In my case, I was successful in acquiring the right-to-use for the screen shots, otherwise I would have had to delete them and replace them with verbal explanations and directions. In other cases, you may have to drop entire sections from your book in order to remain 'legal'. It's simply not worth being sued for copyright infringement.

The next most important item is an International Standard Book Number, commonly referred to as an ISBN. Each book and format combination requires a unique ISBN. In our case we are going to publish several formats of our book. One will be a softcover paper version (one ISBN required). We are also going to publish in several eBook formats: EPUB (a second ISBN), which is the most generic electronic book format and thus the most commonly used, MOBI (a third ISBN) which is the standard format used by the Amazon Kindle Reader, and PDF (a forth ISBN), the Adobe Reader standard format.

Other formats that we could publish in include: the old Sony reader format (LRF), the old Palm format (PDB), HTML for online viewing, the standardized rich text format (RTF) and plain and simple unformatted text (TXT). One of the publishers we use will produce all of these 'old' formats, but I don't bother with them anymore because they've pretty much dropped out of use. But we still need a minimum of four ISBN's. If you wish to publish in the secondary formats you will need more ISBN's, one for each format.

There are several options for acquiring ISBN's. I'm Canadian, so I can apply to the Canadian ISBN Service System (CISS) at: (www.collectionscanada.gc.ca/ciss-ssci/app/index.php?&lang=eng)

and they'll allocate a block of ten numbers, issued to me personally. In Canada there is no charge for acquiring ISBNs. If I use all ten numbers I can apply for more. After publishing my first book in all the available formats, I'd used nine of my ten ISBNs. As I was already planning on a number of subsequent books I requested a block of one hundred to be assigned to me, which, after some discussion, was issued. At the time I had planned on publishing all my books in all nine formats and therefore assumed I needed nine ISBNs per book. I've since dropped back to only four per book, as I don't believe it's worth using the old-style formats anymore. I assumed then that my hundred ISBNs should last me for a little while. However, since publishing my first book, and subsequently writing and publishing nine more books, I have so many ideas for books I'm using up my one hundred numbers much faster than originally anticipated. In Canada the issue, tracking and management of your ISBNs is all done by you via their web site.

If you're American and want your own ISBN's you'll have to purchase them. (Sorry.) They can be acquired from www.Bowker.com. For other countries, I'm afraid you'll have to do your own research to find out how you get ISBN's in your own name. But don't worry, read on.

If you're only publishing one or two books, and don't wish to pay for ISBNs (remember, our mandate here is zero cost), you can simply use the ISBNs offered by the publishers. Two of the three publishers we'll use here will issue an ISBN to your book on your behalf. They don't charge for this so you don't actually have to acquire your own if you don't want to. The difference is that if you use your own numbers as supplied to you by CISS Canada or Bowker, you can list yourself as the publisher and put your own logo on the back cover of your books. If you use the publisher supplied ISBNs, then they are listed as the publisher on the back of the book. As far as I've been able to tell, that's the only difference and has no effect on ownership of the copyright of your book. The copyright remains with you. In order to be published and posted for sale on the international sales sites, your book must have an ISBN (except for Amazon Kindle). It's not optional. Below is an example of how I list my ISBN's in my books.

ISBN: 978-0-9867556-1-3   **Softcover**
ISBN: 978-0-9867556-2-0   .mobi format
ISBN: 978-0-9867556-0-6   .EPUB format
ISBN: 978-0-9867556-5-1   .pdf format
ISBN: 978-0-9867556-3-7   .lrf format
ISBN: 978-0-9867556-4-4   .pdb format
ISBN: 978-0-9867556-6-8   .rtf format
ISBN: 978-0-9867556-7-5   .txt format
ISBN: 978-0-9867556-9-9   .html format

I found it was simpler to put all of the ISBN's in the text of the book rather than having one version of the book for each ISBN. When dealing with multiple versions and multiple formats you would end up with a minimum of four copies of your book, and possibly up to nine, so it's best to keep the number of master copies to the absolute minimum. More on this when we start publishing. In those cases where I have to have a unique copy, I will bold the ISBN specific to that copy. For example, the softcover paperback I create using CreateSpace will have the softcover ISBN bolded. The KDP Kindle version will have the .mobi format line bolded. In the case of Smashwords, I bold the .epub version ISBN.

A second number which is useful but optional is the Cataloguing In Publication number, or CIP. Like ISBNs, CIPs are issued by the home country of the author. Assigning a CIP to your book means that your book is added to the national archives. This means you and your book information go into a national database and a paper copy of the book is stored in the national archives. Pretty heady stuff!

The upside of a CIP is that your book is now in the national archives. The downside is that you're now <u>required</u> to send one, and in some cases two, physical copies of each book to the archive, at your own cost. If you sell less than 100 copies you are required to send one copy of your book to the archive. If you sell more than 100 copies you are required to send two copies. Not a big deal if you're selling thousands of books. A slightly bigger deal if you only sell 10 or 20, as it cuts into your profit margin. I found that the cost of shipping my book to the national archive was more than my profit on two books. Happily, assigning a CIP to your book is optional.

I did get a CIP it for my first two books, so, 'Yay!, I'm in the Canadian National Archives'. I didn't bother with my subsequent books. If (when!) they become best sellers I'll probably reconsider. The other thing with the CIP is that it must be displayed in the front matter of your book, on the copyright page, exactly as formatted by the issuing body. You can use a smaller text and delete blank lines, but that's it. Below is an example of how you place the CIP number in your book.

Library and Archives Canada Cataloguing in Publication
Norton, Stephen C.
     The Marseille scrolls / Stephen C. Norton.
Includes bibliographical references.
Issued also in electronic formats.
ISBN 978-0-9867556-1-3

     I. Title.
PS8627.O796M37 2011   C813'.6   C2011-906170-8

The next item is possibly the most important item for you personally, and that's the copyright statement. Strangely enough, acquiring the copyright statement is actually the easiest part of the whole process. In order to copyright anything that you write, you simply add the text

Copyright © Stephen C Norton 2010

to your document.

However, when publishing the book there is a generally accepted standard layout for the 'copyright page' which includes the copyright statement, the ISBNs and the CIP, along with general disclaimers. The copyright page should be a single page, so you may have to adjust the font size. Below is a typical copyright page, in my standard Bookman Old Style font but at 9 point size. This page is taken from my book **'The Marseille Scrolls'**. Northwind Ink is the name of my publishing company. Note that copyright pages are always complete, single pages. If your copyright page extends over more than a single page you should re-format it or change the font size and line spacing to compress it into a single page.

Example Copyright Page

Published by Stephen Norton at NorthwindInk

Copyright © Stephen C Norton 2010

ISBN: 978-0-9867556-1-3 Softcover
ISBN: 978-0-9867556-2-0   .mobi format
ISBN: 978-0-9867556-0-6   .EPUB format
ISBN: 978-0-9867556-5-1   .pdf format
ISBN: 978-0-9867556-3-7   .lrf format
ISBN: 978-0-9867556-4-4   .pdb format
ISBN: 978-0-9867556-6-8   .rtf format
ISBN: 978-0-9867556-7-5   .txt format
ISBN: 978-0-9867556-9-9   .html format

NorthwindInk Edition, License Notes

Library and Archives Canada Cataloguing in Publication

Norton, Stephen C.
The Marseille scrolls / Stephen C. Norton.

Includes bibliographical references.
Issued also in electronic formats.
ISBN 978-0-9867556-1-3

I. Title.
PS8627.O796M37 2011   C813'.6   C2011-906170-8

There are several other registrations and numbers you can apply for or register with, but as far as I've been able to tell from all my research, all the others are optional. Some of these optional items include the Library of Congress Control Number (LCCN) for US publications. You can also register your copyright, at least in the States, which costs about $30 plus two copies of your book. If you're self-printing and self-selling (we're not) you need a barcode for the back cover of the book. If you buy them, they're about $15-$30 each. In our case they're supplied by our publishers at, you guessed it, no cost. You can also get a UPC code, which can cost $300 or more each, which some do-it-yourself sales sites require (ours don't). You can also register in a multitude of other places. Again, as far as I can tell, they are all optional.

The key items that you must have to publish your book on any of the three sites I'm showing you are: free and clear ownership of the contents of your book, an ISBN for each format and the copyright statement. All the rest are optional, at your choice.

One of the optional things you will probably want to add is a legal disclaimer. Depending on the type of book you're publishing that disclaimer may be simple or fairly complex. The basic disclaimer, which for fictional novels normally appears on the copyright page, looks something like this:

This is a work of fiction. Names, characters, historical events and incidents are either products of the authors imagination or are used fictitiously. Any resemblance to actual persons living or dead, is entirely coincidental. The author has no control over nor responsibility for third party web sites or their content.

For other types of books, such as a 'how-to' book where you're talking about use of tools and safety, or this book where you're making recommendations which could have legal liability, you may want your disclaimer to be something a little more detailed. An easy way to build your disclaimer statement the way you want it is to do a scan of the Internet for disclaimer statements and, after reviewing several, build one to meet your own personal requirements. An example of one I've built for my own use is shown below.

<u>Example Disclaimer Page</u>

Disclaimer

The purpose of this book is to provide information, educate and entertain. Whilst every care has been taken in preparing the information contained in this book, neither the author nor the publisher guarantees the accuracy or currency of the content.

By using this book, you are agreeing to the following conditions:

You expressly acknowledge that neither the author nor the publisher can be held responsible for any errors or omissions and accept no liability whatsoever for any loss or damage howsoever arising from, or alleged to have been caused, directly or indirectly, by the use of this book or its contents. Use of this book and its content is entirely at your own risk.

You expressly acknowledge that all content within this book and all services provided or described within it are provided "as is", with no guarantees of completeness, accuracy or timeliness, and without representations, warranties or other contractual terms of any kind, express or implied. The author and the publisher reserve the right to remove or alter content within this book at any time without notice. All services and offerings described are subject to change without notice.

You expressly acknowledge that neither the author nor the publisher has any control over, or responsibility for, the content or privacy practices of any Internet site listed within this book. These sites are provided to you as a convenience and the inclusion of any site link does not in any way imply endorsement by the author or the publisher.

~~~~

Technical Complexity: low

Accessing web sites to acquire ISBNs and other registrations if desired.

Publishing Routes

So you've just finished writing the world's next great book. A novel, perhaps a fictional mystery, perhaps a literary book, or maybe even a riveting memoir. It doesn't matter. Whatever it is you're sure it will take the world by storm. But in order to take the world by storm, you must first get it out into the world. You must publish the book. This involves finding a publisher to print and distribute the book for you. I've found that there are four possible routes to getting your book published.

The **'Traditional'** route to publishing is one that we all know. First, the author connects directly with the publishing house or, much more likely today, with an agent. The agent then takes your document and offers it to a variety of publishing houses. One or more of the publishing houses offer the agent a bid on the book, and you and your agent select the publishing house you wish to go with. Contracts are signed, you get an upfront advance payment of anywhere from one to several thousand dollars. The publisher publishes the book and you are paid a royalty on the sale of each copy of the book.

You don't get paid anything more than the advance until the royalties due exceed the original payment. The payments you do get for your book will usually be in the realm of five to seven percent of the retail cover price of the book. From that payment your agent will then take their ten to fifteen percent. This may even go to twenty or twenty-five percent, depending on the agent you linked up with. The remainder goes to you. Let's put some real numbers on that.

The standard paperback or 6" x 9" softcover fiction novel currently sells for about $12.99. From that, your royalty at 7% is $0.91 per book. From that $0.91 your agent collects $0.14, leaving you with a grand total of $0.77 per book sold. Let's be very generous and say the publishing house offered you a $5,000 advance payment. That means you're going to need to sell almost six thousand five hundred books before you start making any additional money.

Now let's look at some general publishing statistics. An average book in the traditional publishing environment has a lifespan on the bookshelves of anywhere from 3 to 6 months, unless you're already a major established author. So a new author can expect a maximum of six months. Given the number of books currently available on the market, the total sales volume of an average book ranges anywhere from 500 to 1,000 copies. That's considered a reasonably successful first book. As you can see that's a lot less than the required 6,500 books. Still, let's follow this process through.

First, like so many authors before you, you scan the web pages of all the major publishing houses, only to find that none of them give you any idea of how to contact them. You have just discovered harsh fact number one. In the publishing industry of today, publishing houses no longer wish to speak directly to authors, and certainly not new, unknown, authors. In fact, the large majority of publishing houses will only speak to agents, and more and more commonly, only to agents they have successfully dealt with in the past. Note the emphasis on successfully. In fact, it seems the publishing house of today only wishes to publish books written by well-known, successful authors who have already published and successfully sold several books. New York bestseller authors are prime targets. You, the new guy on the block with no track record, are not a prime target. In fact you are not even a target, you're a risk.

So if you can't talk to the publishing houses without an agent you must now find an agent. So, once again you go back to the Internet to scan the web pages of all the agents you can find. Most agent web pages do at least give you directions on how to contact them, along with directions on how to send them your document for review. One problem though, these days many agents have signs on their web pages saying they're only working with existing, successful clients. But there are agents out there willing to take on new clients if they like a book. So develop an outline of the book or an overview depending on what the agent wants, enclose the first two, five, ten or fifty pages of your book, whatever is required and send it to the agent along with a stamped self addressed envelope. That last requirement does make things a little difficult if you don't live in the country where the agent is. I'm in Canada, and buying American stamps and having them delivered to a Canadian address is difficult to say the least. Many agents also request / require 'exclusive' review periods. That is, you send them a copy of your manuscript for review and promise not to send it to anyone else for a certain time period. Those time periods can be anywhere from six weeks to six months. This means your book can be tied up in limbo with a single agent for up to six months, until the agent gets around to reviewing it. Odds are very good that at the end of the six months you will receive your self-addressed envelope with a little note inside saying thanks, but no thanks. Very rarely, you may get a short note explaining why the agent is not prepared to take you on. Very, very rarely, you may get a note offering some critique or suggestion on how to make the book more attractive to the agent. You really can't blame the agents, as I'm quite sure they get inundated with documents for review, and if they're going to make money they obviously have to pick only the very best of the best. Again, a new, untried author isn't a gold mine. He or she is unproven, and therefore a risk.

Quite literally, years can go by while you try to find an agent. I spent almost two and a half years searching for an agent willing to take on my first book before I finally gave up on this route. If you do actually succeed in finding an agent, a few more years can potentially go by while the agent finds a publisher willing to bankroll the publication of your book. A rough ballpark estimate is that for every thousand new authors, perhaps one will actually get published. For every thousand that gets published, only a very, very few go on to appear on the new York Times Best Seller List. Quite a depressing statistic considering you're full of enthusiasm for that book you've just finished.

That's the classic route, and I will leave it there. I had no success with it. But, all is not quite lost. There are self-publishing routes available to you which avoid the anguish of hunting for agents and publishers, so let's look at these.

The next route, which at one point had a fair amount of popularity, was the original self-publishing route, more commonly called '**Vanity Publishing**'. The vanity publisher was just that. It was a process by which the publisher preyed on the author's vanity with the offer of publishing his or her book. The publisher would offer a series of services which would assist the author in preparing their manuscript for publication. All of these services cost money and all of them were required in order for the author to get the book published. At the end of it all the author would be able to purchase copies of their book from the publisher 'at cost'. The only trouble was the cost of an individual book was exceedingly high, often more than double or triple any possible book cover price the author could charge. There was often also a minimum publishing number, meaning the author was required to order twenty, fifty or in some cases up to five hundred copies of their book in order to get any. The usual result of the vanity publishing route was that the author would pay anywhere from five to fifteen thousand dollars or more and end up with several boxes of books in their basement, waiting for someone to personally sell them. For the majority of authors the vanity publisher was really not much more than a con artist. You paid a lot, you got a bunch of books, but you had no distributor and no way to market or sell your books.

The other route open to the new author was the '**Self-Printing**' route, where the author did all of the required publishing tasks themselves. There were many books written on how to pursue this route, all giving detailed lists of tools required and tasks to be done. Some of these tasks were things like purchasing and learning software to do page layout and typographical setting. A popular package here was Adobe's PageMaker, which also allowed you to output a PDF document. PageMaker was always a fairly expensive and complex software package, though it was definitely an excellent tool for page layout. The downside was it was also quite hard to master. Now it's become InDesign it's even more expensive and complex to use. Other packages you could require included things like FrontPage or Dreamweaver for building and maintaining your sales Web, something like Microsoft Publisher for producing sales brochures, newsletters and other promotional materials, an accounting package for keeping track of costs, sales, inventory control, invoicing, receipts, payments etc. You also needed a photographic tool for managing images in your book, book covers, promotional pictures, brochure photos and business logos. Some of the older books detailing how to self-print / self-publish also recommended acquiring and using mass e-mail tools, something that we now refer to as spam. Because you would be producing your own brochures and handouts you also needed a good quality color printer. At this point you've probably invested one to two thousand dollars in software and equipment, possibly a lot more.

Going this route also required the author to learn a lot of new skills, all unrelated to writing. This obviously took a great deal of time away from the author's task of actually writing a book. You'd create your book in your word processor, import it into the page layout tool, create a galley format which could then be taken down to a local printer where you would then pay to have draft copies of the book printed. One recommendation was to print off perhaps one hundred copies of your galley book for circulation to others for editing, critiques and reviews. After collecting the critiques and reviews and making any recommended modifications to your original document, you would then create another galley ready for printing and have your local printer produce some number of books which you would then sell.

Most local printers at that time had a minimum run volume of anywhere from five hundred to two thousand copies. Similar to the vanity publisher, this meant that the author would end up with several cases of books in his or her basement waiting to be sold. Common pricing for the galley book of one hundred copies would be five to seven dollars per copy, due to the low volume, so there's at least five hundred dollars for the galley books. The first production run, say one thousand copies, would probably cost around three fifty per copy (larger volume discount), so there's another thirty-five hundred dollars. If you were producing a hardcover book the minimum print run numbers were probably about the same, but the cost per book would be somewhere in the range of ten dollars a copy. So, going this self-printing / self-publishing route, you spent some fifteen hundred on software and equipment, five hundred to one thousand for galley proofs and anywhere from thirty-five to ten thousand for production runs.

Now, just like the vanity publishing route, you had to sell all of the books you had printed. This required the author to learn yet more skills, those of marketing and sales, again taking time away from the writing process. There are innumerable books written and sold on how to go this route and many people did choose to go this route. I'm fairly certain that the only people who made any money were the people writing the books on how to self-print and self-publish and the printers. Like the vanity publishing route, the end result was most likely to be an author, some five to ten thousand dollars poorer, with several cases of books sitting in their basement, waiting for someone to sell them.

Marketing is a on-going issue, regardless of which route you go. Even the traditional publishing houses now expect the author to do most, if not all, the sales and marketing. I'll leave marketing for later on, but we will get to it.

The new route to true '**Self-publishing**' appeared on the Internet around 2007. It takes the form of websites which accept a Word document from the author, convert it into a published format and then either post it on their own website for sale or distribute it to other bookselling websites.

To my knowledge, this started with a company called Smashwords, which focused on producing eBooks. Over the years Smashwords developed relationships with many of the major companies and thus took on both the publishing and distribution tasks for the author. The author established an account on the Smashwords website, submitted their book, authorized publication and carried on writing their next book. The Smashwords web site sold the books via the Internet, took their cut, and placed the authors portion in an account. On some regular schedule Smashwords would then forward the author's royalty payment to the author via either a bank account electronic funds transfer, if the author was in the States, or via a PayPal transfer for authors outside the States. This relieved the author of all of the publishing, marketing, sales and billing tasks, removed the requirement for purchasing and learning a multitude of software packages and acquiring fancy printers, while paying the author a much higher percentage of the cover price of each book. Best of all, no up-front payment was required of the author.

Smashwords, to my knowledge, was and remains the leader in this field, allowing the author to produce eBooks quickly, easily and in multiple formats. They were soon followed by other companies including Amazon, which has a process for producing .mobi format eBooks for the Kindle, and an Amazon subsidiary called CreateSpace, which produces softcover paper books. The general process remains the same across all three sites. The author registers with the site at no cost, submits their document to the website, the website converts it as appropriate to produce a given format, be it eBook or paper, and the company distributes the book to one or more book seller web sites for sale. The author receives royalties on any subsequent sales and sees a much higher per book percentage of the sales price. This leaves the author free to focus on writing and marketing his books.

What I'm going to do is walk you through my personal journey of how I publish my books. I've already described my trials with the traditional publishing route. I investigated vanity publishing and discarded it as basically a con game. I read many books and took several courses on how to do self-publishing using the self-printing method described above and came to the conclusion it was just too expensive and require too big an upfront investment, of both my time and my money.

One of the courses I took was a one-day session on how to use Smashwords, and that's where I started. Over time I discovered CreateSpace, and a little later the Amazon Kindle Direct Publishing (KDP) site. I'd finally discovered a practical route to self-publishing, one which I could afford. A route which gave me the ability to have my book published, on my terms, on my schedule, at zero cost to me, while still having it distributed to well known and generally accepted worldwide marketplaces. What I'd like to do now is take you on that journey as we walk through the three web sites offering free publishing of your book. Hopefully walking you through my journey will shorten your journey by years of frustration and many, many rejection letters, plus save you a large amount of money, while allowing you to publish your book in an easy and timely manner. Hopefully you'll also get to collect some royalties too.

We've covered a lot of ground so far so let's just quickly review the expected cost of the book from the four routes I've outlined. Following the traditional route, for your very first book, it can take years to find an agent and then more years to get it sold to a publisher. Your likely advance will probably not exceed one thousand dollars or so, and that's being pretty optimistic. Your royalty payments will most likely be in the range of five percent of the cover price, less the fifteen to twenty-five percent agent fees. And you won't see any income beyond your advance until your royalty payments exceed the advance amount. Given the average sales of a book these days, some sources suggest a new authors successful book will most likely sell no more than five hundred to one thousand copies before being driven off the market by other books. This assumes you actually find an agent and a publishing house both willing to take a risk on your new book.

Following the vanity press route, the cost of your book will be more than you really should be willing to pay just to see it in print. Your cost, as much as you'll pay, your royalty.... er, never heard of anyone seeing one. Vanity presses sell you your own books at very close to what reality says is your actual maximum sale price, sometimes even more, so your potential profit margin is probably nonexistent or negative. All the profits from your book go to the vanity press, not to you. That's essentially why they're called vanity presses. I've been given to understand that a print run of one hundred copies can cost anywhere from three to five thousand dollars, though I have to admit that's just what I've been able to glean from their web site sales pitches.

If you follow the third route and take on the onerous tasks involved in printing it yourself, your costs are surprisingly similar to the vanity press route. One reputable Canadian printer now offers self-publishing packages. A basic black-and-white paperback package starts at six hundred dollars, and gives you five copies of your book. The high-end black-and-white package goes for twenty-four hundred dollars and includes fifteen paperbacks, five hardback copies and two eBook formats. Full color book packages go for three thousand dollars and give you up to two revisions, two hours of book promotion coaching and up to fifteen paperbacks and five hardbacks. Marketing packages are sold separately, with prices ranging from six hundred to three thousand dollars. Your total cost, somewhere between five and ten thousand dollars for a reasonable print production run. Your royalty, well, after you've become a successful salesman, sold a thousand books or more and recovered your initial investment....

The fourth route is to do it yourself using this book as a guide. Your minimum cost is the cost of this book, plus your own time to implement the instructions. Your most likely maximum total cost, including the cost of this book, a couple of printed paper proof copies and shipping, is less than fifty dollars. Your royalties range from thirty-five to seventy percent of the cover price you set on the book. Your sales distribution area is international, with your books being offered from book sellers such as Amazon, Apple, Barnes & Noble, Kobo and others.

Why are these 'new' companies different? Why do they do it 'for free'? Because you can make money for them, while they're helping you make money for yourself. Their up-front investment is fairly low, especially once they have their web site set up and the conversion tools implemented. Adding the five hundredth author is almost a zero cost to them, while adding that five hundredth order simply adds another profit stream to their accounts. Happily, adding that five hundredth order also adds a profit stream to your account as well.

Now, let's begin publishing our book!

Building Your Paper Book

I've mentioned three different publishing groups, Smashwords, CreateSpace, and Amazon, that we're going to use. I've also said that I started with Smashwords, which is the multi-format eBook publishing site. That was where I started with my very first published book, but I've since found that, as you have to build what is essentially the paper version in order to write the book, it actually makes the most sense to publish that version first. The paper version is produced using the CreateSpace process.

The reason for this is that the paper version requires the most structure and formatting, and having a printed version makes the final editing much easier. Thus I found it's easier to start with the most complex document, get that published and then strip out whatever is required to publish in the less complex environments. This ensures that your true master document is the most complex one and all the others versions fall out reasonably cleanly from the original master. Thus we're going to start by creating a book formatted for our soft cover paper version, and publish it using CreateSpace.

The first thing you need to do is go to CreateSpace at www.CreateSpace.com, create yourself an account and sign in. The next thing you need to do is decide what size format you're going to use to publish your book. This book size / format is referred to as the 'trim size'. This is largely dictated by your page size, which in turn is dictated by the contents of your book. For example, in my 'how-to' books I wanted to present a large number of photographs. I also wanted them displayed in the book so they were large enough to be easily read and yet small enough that I could fit the most pictures into the fewest pages.

This is important because the cost of your book is dictated by two things, the fixed costs and the variable costs. The fixed costs cover the basic setup, book size, interior paper color and whether the book is printed in black and white or full color. The variable cost is the number of pages to be printed and is dependent on the number of words, number of pictures, font size and line spacing. Thus, regardless of the cover price you assign to your book, the actual cost of production will be dictated by the number of pages of your book and whether they're black-and-white or color. When it comes to selling, you put a cover price on your book and the cost of actual production is the first thing subtracted from your cover price. Because my 'how-to' books would be printed in full color, with many reasonably large pictures, the best price per page cost meant they fit best within an 8 x 10 format. That format size was also the most obvious for a book which would be used as a guide in the workshop.

On the other hand, my novel was simply black-and-white text with no pictures and so could have been either a standard paperback size of approximately 5" x 8", or the newer format for paperbacks which is a 6" x 9" format. Keeping the font and line spacing static, the number of pages of each size is dictated by the format, so a standard 5" x 8" paperback size results in more pages than the newer 6" x 9" format. More pages would have increased my costs, while my best possible cover price was dictated by industry standard pricing for novels and was therefore essentially fixed, regardless of the format size I used. If I push my cover price beyond the industry standard it decreases my likelihood of sales. The general public expects to pay $12.99 for a paperback novel, and so would be unlikely to pay $14.99 for my novel. As a result I chose the 6" x 9" format for my novels. I've also published several memoirs for other people, basically black-and-white text with a few color pictures, and again the 6" x 9" format made the most sense. The 6" x 9" format seems to be slowly becoming the industry standard now, probably because of the issues I've just outlined.

CreateSpace supports a large number of industry standard trim sizes and provides blank and pre-filled Word templates for each size selection. The easiest way to deal with formatting your book correctly is to download the appropriate template and then import your document into the template. Just remember when you're importing to do a 'Paste Special' and paste as 'Unformatted Text', otherwise you will import the formatting from your draft document, which will mess up the template formatting. The pre-filled templates are, in my opinion, the most useful when you're first starting out, as they provide 'position appropriate' text on the pages and you can thus see which page should be the title, table of contents, copyright page, dedications, acknowledgements etc. and which the body text of the book. When you cut and paste your text into position you can simply over-write the example text.

Listed below are the Word page setup parameters for a 6" x 9" format from CreateSpace's blank template. (File, Page Setup, from Word's Menu bar.)

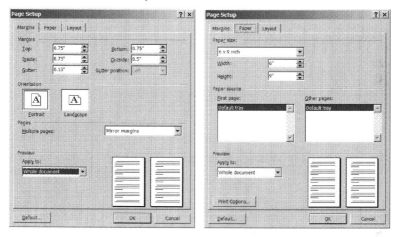

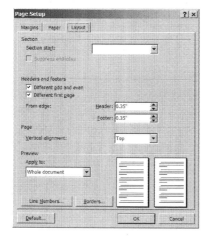

Below are the paragraph settings for the same 6" x 9" format.

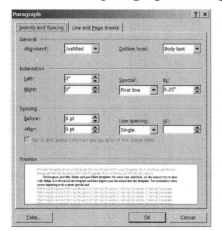
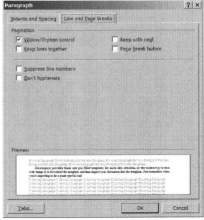

Alternatively, if you don't want the first line of each paragraph indented, but do want a little extra space between paragraphs, you can use this paragraph format, with 6 points of space left after a paragraph end. For novels I use the indent format, while for 'how-to' books I use the no-indent format.

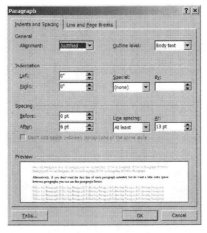

Probably one of the most important issues when writing a book is the font that you use. There are a huge number of fonts available and it can be difficult to decide which font to use. Searching the web for recommended fonts to be used in printed books returns a plethora of responses and you could almost write a book on font selection alone. I'm sure someone has somewhere. The reason font selection is so critical is because a good font can make the book easier to read and thus provide an enjoyable environment for the reader. A font which is too small or difficult to make out on the page can lead to headaches and / or eyestrain, making your book less attractive to the reader. 'I really liked the story line, but the font was very hard on my eyes, so I stopped reading half-way through.'

The key item to consider is whether to use a **serif** font or a **sans serif** font. A serif font is a typeface with small finishing strokes at the beginning and end of each letter. The text you're reading uses a serif font. They are designed this way as the eye tends to follow the finishing strokes and continue on smoothly to the next letter. This tends to result in easier eye movement and thus less eyestrain when reading large amounts of text on paper. (At least that's what the font research books say.) A sans serif font lacks this ornamentation and is designed more for simplicity and a modernistic or minimalist feel. General consensus is that a serif font is best used in the body of your book, while sans serif fonts are more useful on computer monitor screens, though they are also sometimes recommended for book covers and title pages.

Examples of serif fonts commonly used in book texts include Georgia, Book Antigua, Garamond, Minion and Bookman. Examples of commonly used sans serif fonts include Helvetica, Arial, Verdana and Tahoma. There are a couple of other classes of fonts, one of which is **script** font which includes things like Monotype Corsiva, Edwardian Script, Lucinda Handwriting and Brush Script. The script fonts are designed to emulate cursive handwriting and while they're very elegant in small doses they should only be used on book covers and titles, never in the body text. In a large font size, a script font adds a touch of elegance, and thus makes the title more attractive to the eye. In smaller font sizes such as the 10 or 12 point sizes commonly used in the books interior text, the script fonts become almost unreadable.

As I mentioned, there are thousands of fonts out there on the Internet, some available for free download, while others are purchasable, with prices that can run anywhere from fifteen dollars for a font set up to one thousand or more. The reason there are so many fonts is that many of the new fonts are based on old fonts, with slight modifications or changes intended to improve the font or customize it to someone's personal style. There is no need to purchase a font for your book. There is an excellent selection available in the standard Windows font set, and lots of free font sets available for download from the Internet.

My preferred font for the interior text is Bookman Old Style, in 11 or 12 point size. Bookman was based on Old Style Antique, which was in turn designed as a replacement for the older Caslon font and thus has many similarities to Caslon. My preferred fonts for my title page are Edwardian Script ITC in 48 point size for the title and Monotype Corsiva in 28 point size for the authors name. I found that my name, in Edwardian Script at the 28 point size, was quite difficult to read on paper.

All other text within my books are Bookman Old Style in various point sizes ranging from 9 point for the CIP and copyright page, 11 or 12 point for the interior text, and 13 or 14 point for the chapter headings. I use the regular font for the most part, with **bolding,** *italics* and <u>underlined</u> reserved for particular emphasis. The general recommendation when using a serif font for the body text is to go no smaller than 10 point. If you do choose to use a sans serif font for the body text the recommendation is no smaller than 8 point and size.

One thing that is recommended across the board is to avoid the use of too many fonts within the text body. One, two or possibly three fonts used in the book interior is acceptable. Any more than that distracts the viewer from the text and thus defeats the purpose of having an attractive, easy to read font.

It is impossible to properly evaluate fonts intended for book texts on a computer screen. When comparing various fonts for your selection you must print them off on a good quality printer and compare the paper output, not the on-screen output. CreateSpace provides online proofing tools, allowing you to actually see the final 'printed' version of your book on-screen, and thus do all of your proofing and approvals via the computer screen. However, I strongly recommend getting at least one printed paper proof so you can see exactly what your book will look like when your customers purchase it. Having that 'real' book in your hands, and being able to see the print on paper simply cannot be replaced by your computer screen. I've also found I capture more edit errors where reviewing a 'real' paper book than I do when reviewing an electronic version.

Below is a list from the CreateSpace support website, showing the various fonts for book interiors as recommended by a variety of other websites and book related organizations.

~~~~~~~~~~~~~~~~~~~~~

Fontfeed: Minion, ITC New Baskerville, FF Scala, FF Scala Sans, Adobe Garamond, Trade Gothic, Electra, Fournier, Dante, Din

Self-Pub: Times New Roman, Garamond, Bookman Old Style, Book Antiqua

Linotype: Stemple Garamond, Times Ten, ITC Weidemann, Sabon Next, Palatino, LinoLetter, Fairfield, Linotype Camptil, Linotype Finnegan, Trajanus

The Bookdesigner: Garamond, Janson, Bembo, Caslon, Electra

Ezinearticles: Palatino, Book Antiqua, Georgia, Adobe Garamond, Bookman, Century Schoolbook

Fontshop: ITC New Baskerville, FF Scala, Minion Pro, Electra, Adobe Garamond, Dante, Bembo Book

~~~~~~~~~~~~~~~~~~~~~

As you can see, there is not a great deal of common agreement, so you'll have to make your own decision.

An integral part of the font size is the line spacing. The US hardcover and trade paperback industry standards recommend line spacing of 120% to 125% of the font size. This means a book interior in Bookman Old Style 11 point font should have either 13.2 or 13.75 point line spacing. Specifying your line spacing to this level is probably a little more sophisticated than you really need to get, as the Word default of single space is usually a reasonable choice. However if you so desire you can specify in the Word paragraph setup exactly the line spacing you want. To really evaluate your chosen spacing though, you still need a paper proof copy. To access the setup for line spacing in Word, click on 'Format' on the Menu bar and then take the 'Paragraph' option. On the screenshots below the left hand side indicates Word's standard single space, and on the right-hand side I have specified my preferred spacing.

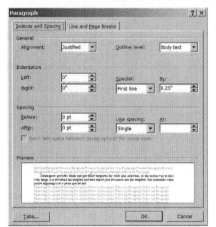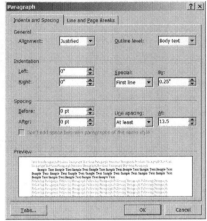

For those interested in producing a Large Print version, the American Printing House for the Blind (APH) has developed some standard guidelines. In fact they've even produced their own font, the APHont, which can be downloaded from their website (www.aph.org). Their general recommendations are that large print should be at least 16 point and preferably 18 point. Interestingly they recommend sans serif fonts for the body of the text including fonts such as APHont, Antique Olive, Helvetica, Plantin, Tahoma and Verdana. They also recommend spacing of 1.5 between lines and double spacing between paragraphs, left justified with a ragged right margin and with no indents.

This is almost the complete opposite of the industry-standard recommendations for regular print versions, which specify justified margins, single lines between paragraphs and indents on the first line of the paragraph.

Some examples of various fonts are listed below, all shown at 10 point with single spacing. The descriptions are taken from within the font files themselves.

~~~~

Arial 10
Contemporary sans serif design, Arial contains more humanist characteristics than many of its predecessors and as such is more in tune with the mood of the last decades of the twentieth century. *The overall treatment of curves is softer and fuller than in most industrial style sans serif faces.* Terminal strokes are cut on the diagonal which helps to give the face a less mechanical appearance. Arial is an extremely versatile family of typefaces which can be used with equal.

Bookman Old Style 10
The origins of Bookman Old Style lie in the typeface called Oldstyle Antique, designed by A C Phemister circa 1858 for the Miller and Richard foundry in Edinburgh, Scotland. *Many American foundries made versions of this type which eventually became known as Bookman.* Monotype Bookman Old Style roman is based on earlier Lanston Monotype and ATF models. The italic has been re drawn following the style of the Oldstyle Antique italics of Miller and Richard. Although called 'Old Style', the near vertical stress of the face puts it into the transitional category. A legible and robust text face.

Book Antiqua 10
This is a roman typeface based on pen-drawn letters of the Italian Renaissance. Because it is distinctive and gentle in appearance it can be used to give a document *a different feel than is given by the more geometrical designs of most text faces.* It is also useful for occasional lines, as in letter headings and compliments slips. Its beautiful italic has many uses of its own.

Garamond 10
Monotype Drawing Office 1922. This typeface is based on roman types cut by Jean Jannon in 1615. Jannon followed the designs of Claude Garamond which had been cut in the previous century. *Garamond's types were, in turn, based on those used by Aldus Manutius in 1495 and cut by Francesco Griffo.* The italic is based on types cut in France circa 1557 by Robert Granjon. Garamond is a beautiful typeface with an air of informality which looks good in a wide range of applications. It works particularly well in books and lengthy text settings.

Tahoma 10
Tahoma is one of Microsoft's new sans serif typeface families. It consists of two Windows TrueType fonts (regular and bold), and was created to address the challenges of on-screen display, particularly at small sizes in dialog boxes and menus.
Since the Tahomas are TrueType fonts, they can be rotated and scaled to any size, and anti-aliased by the rasterizer built into Microsoft Windows 95

and Microsoft Windows NT 4.0. These features give the fonts significant advantages over bitmap system fonts such as MS Sans Serif.

Times New Roman 10
This remarkable typeface first appeared in 1932 in The Times of London newspaper, for which it was designed. It has subsequently become one of the worlds most successful type creations. *The original drawings were made under Stanley Morison's direction by Victor Lardent at The Times. It then went through an extensive iterative process involving further work in Monotype's Type Drawing Office.* Based on experiments Morison had conducted using Perpetua and Plantin, it has many old style characteristics but was adapted to give excellent legibility coupled with good economy. Widely used in books and magazines, for reports, office documents and also for display and advertising.

Verdana 10
The Verdana typeface family was designed specifically to address the challenges of on-screen display. Designed by world renowned type designer Matthew Carter, and hand-instructed by leading hinting expert, Monotype's Tom Rickner, these sans serif fonts are unique examples of type design for the computer screen. *In its proportions and stroke weight, the Verdana family resembles sans serifs such as Frutiger, and Johnston's typeface for the London Underground.*
The Verdana fonts are stripped of features which are redundant when applied to the screen. They exhibit new characteristics, derived from the pixel rather than the pen, the brush or the chisel. The balance between straight, curve and diagonal has been meticulously tuned to ensure that the pixel patterns at small sizes are pleasing, clear and legible.

~~~~

Notice that while all of the fonts shown above are 10 point, their actual printed size differs quite substantially. This is why I strongly recommend reviewing your book at least once in paper hardcopy as produced by the printer, so you know exactly what your customers will be seeing.

My very first proof was in Times New Roman 12 point and left justified, because that's how all my technical and business reports had always been done, probably because that was Word's default setting. The printed result in paper book format looked very amateurish. The second proof was in the industry standard recommended 'justified' format (both right and left margin justified, as this book is). I also switched to a recommended book text font, Bookman Old Style which produced a much more professional result. However, I started with the Bookman font at the 10 point size, single spaced, because it looked very nice on screen and on the web page proofing tools. After reading a few chapters of the book's paper proof, I found the 10 point size was small enough to cause me some eye-strain. My next proof was 11 point, with line spacing set to 'at least 13 pt' and that solved the eye-strain problem.

I did order (buy) a number of paper proof prints during the creation of my first novel. Each one was a learning experience. My intent with this book is to help you skip many of the learning mis-steps, so you can produce a high-quality, professional looking book right from the word go.

One last note. Many of these considerations become fairly immaterial when we get to the eBook creation, as most good quality eBook readers all allow the user to adjust their reading font size, and many now allow the user to also specify their own preferred font, font substitution, font size and line spacing.

Conclusions:

- Choose an appropriate page / trim size for your book
- Download the pre-built, pre-filled Word template from CreateSpace
- Add your text to the pre-filled template
- Select an easy-to-read serif font for the book interior
- Use an eye-catching font for your book cover and title page, serif, san serif or script
- Use an easy-on-the eye font size and line spacing for the book interior
- Review your choices from a paper proof copy

Technical Complexity: low to medium

Should have familiarity with Word functions like Page setup, Format, Font and Paragraph styles.

Managing Photographs and Pictures

While implementing the formatting of your document is almost the last thing you do when preparing the book for publishing, one large exception to that statement is pictures and photographs inserted in the body of your document.

Any photographs, scanned images or pictures should be a minimum of three hundred dots per inch (300 dpi) in resolution and should be embedded in the text using Word's 'In line with Text' option. The other options allow the pictures to float around inside the document and any re-formatting of the document is quite likely to change the location of the images, often seemingly randomly. Three hundred dpi is a measure of the resolution of the image, the 'depth of the quality' if you will. Usually, the larger the dpi number, the better quality the picture. Scanners can be manually set to the desired dpi prior to scanning and so are not really a problem.

Cameras on the other hand are a pain, because almost all of them insist on photographing at 72 dpi resolution. The megapixel size doesn't change that, it simply makes bigger images. However, most photo manipulation software will allow you to resize the image and adjust the dpi at the same time. For example, my sixteen megapixel camera takes photos at 72 dpi with an image size of 4608 x 3456 pixels. One of the tools I use, Paint Shop Pro, reports that image size as 64" x 48". My ten megapixel Fuji takes pictures sized to 3648 x 2736 pixels or 50" x 38". My old four megapixel camera took pictures at 2272 x 1712 pixels or 31" x 24". All these cameras store the picture at 72 dpi.

I have found an outstanding photo manipulation tool called FastStone Image Viewer, which lets you resize your picture down to the size you want for your book while simultaneously adjusting the dpi to 300 (or higher if you choose). For books with a lot of photographs, like my 'How-to's', I resize the photos to about 3 1/2 inches wide at 300 dpi, so I can fit two pictures side by side on an 8 inch printed page. You can then click and drag the picture directly from FastStone into your Word document, easily placing the pictures exactly where you want them in the text. I've found this 'easy placement' is essential because you'll sometimes find you end up replacing a series of photos. Doing that one photo at a time is arduous.

I think of FastStone as a compressor, as it takes a big 72 dpi picture and squashes it down to a smaller size but with a higher dpi. There is no loss of detail at all. Think of squeezing a sponge; as it gets squeezed smaller, it becomes denser - the dpi increases. A 72 dpi picture five inches wide, compressed down to one inch wide will become 360 dpi. This means a ten or sixteen megapixel camera gives lots of manoeuvring room for compressing pictures and increasing resolution without loss of quality.

FastStone also does batch processing. I used it in the how-to books to compress, resize and adjust all of the pictures in a chapter at one time, then placed them in the chapter in Word in the appropriate positions. This was much, much easier than any other process I've found for manipulating photos for addition to a book interior.

Although the process sounds complex, management and preparation of your photographs for inclusion in your book is actually fairly simple. First take your photographs. I found that for my books, photographs with a nice clean, white background were best. Make sure you use lots of light. You don't need to have a professional photographers studio with multiple flashes, but a few 150 watt clip-on lights arranged strategically are very useful. Try to minimize both glare and shadows by placing lights on both sides of the object you're photographing, plus possibly overhead and from an angle below. The idea is to evenly flood the subject with light, so there are neither dark shadows nor harsh bright areas.

I also bracket what the camera tells me is the best exposure. That means to slightly overexpose and slightly underexpose your pictures. You actually end up with three copies of the photograph. Some cameras have a setting that will do that automatically referred to as EV +/- 1. Using a digital camera makes this a no-cost issue, as you can take as many photos as you want, then pick out the ones you like best and discard the rest. The book printing process does tend to darken the photos slightly, so I usually overexpose by one stop, and sometimes two. Experiment a bit with both the exposure of the photos and the angles from which they're taken, to get the best photo that clearly explains what you're showing. Always remember that when you see your proof copy, if you don't like what you see, you can always go back and change things. Just make sure you have photographs at different exposures that you can substitute, or good quality pictures you can manipulate. Use of RAW format for the pictures is useful for this, but that level of complexity is more than we really need.

Take all of your photos in full color, even if you intend to use only black and white images in your book. Use your photo manipulation tool (FastStone) to convert the full color image to grayscale, with the number of shades of grey set as high as it will go. This provides you with a much better quality black and white picture than using a grayscale original direct from the camera, as an original full color photo has many more tones than an equivalent grayscale photo. Converting from color to grayscale also provides more flexibility, as you also have the option to play with the colors, hue and saturation etc, both before or after converting to grayscale. The software on your computer will almost always provide a better conversion than the software on your camera. High-end DSLR cameras may be an exception, but those tend to be in the thousand dollar plus range. You can easily do everything you need for publishing with a digital camera in the one to three hundred dollar price range.

Once you've taken some pictures, load your photographs onto your computer, immediately make a working copy of your photographs and put the originals in a separate file folder as backup. This ensures that you have an original copy, so if you mess up during your manipulations you can always revert back to an original. I file my photos by chapter, so for each chapter I have a folder called 'originals', and a second folder called 'for the book'. For any manipulations I do, I then set FastStone to read from the 'originals' folder, do the full batch conversions and write the results out to the 'for the book' folder.

Load your photos into FastStone's Image Viewer, review all the photos you've taken, select the ones you think are most appropriate for your book and move them into the 'originals' folder. You can discard the others, or put them in another folder, out of the way. Using the FastStone 'Tools' menu, select the 'Batch Convert Selected Images' option. Define your output folder to be 'for the book', then open the Advanced options menu. From here you can resize the picture, adjust the dpi and, if desired, convert to grayscale simultaneously for all of the selected images. On the resize menu specify a new width and height for your images so that they will fit comfortably within your chosen page size. A 2" width allows two pictures to sit side-by-side on a 6" wide page with a bit of white space between them. On the dpi screen specify the X and Y dpi settings that you want. I usually set both to 400 dpi. Click Okay to select these options. Then click the convert button. All of the selected images will now be resized, the dpi set to 400 and the results written out to the 'for the book' folder. Once completed click the close button. You can repeat this process with variations as many times as you like, because you're reading from one folder and writing to another.

From the FastStone main display, select the folder where the adjusted images were written to. Open your document and arrange the two windows side by side. You can now click and drag the adjusted images from FastStone directly into your Word document. Depending on your chosen page size you may want to play around with different sizes to find the fit you like the best. It's a much better choice to do the resizing in a photo tool, especially something like FastStone, which does JPEG lossless manipulation, meaning no data or detail is lost, rather than placing the picture into Word first and then resizing it in Word. Word is definitely not a picture manipulation tool.

Be aware that using high dpi images will cause your Word document to get quite large. My 250 page novel, text only, produced a final Word document just under one (1) megabyte in size. My 'how-to' books, loaded with images, produced a Word document over two hundred (200) megabytes in size. This size does reduce when we create the PDF file for upload to CreateSpace and it reduces even more when we compress the images for producing our eBooks. However, most of the size is due to the high definition of the pictures and it's best to keep the original master document with pictures of the highest definition. CreateSpace will give you error messages for any picture less than 300 dpi, so don't reduce anything until you absolutely have to.

If you're using pictures to demonstrate a process or action and you want to embed arrows in the photo, for example, pointing to a specific tool or specific point in the photograph, do not use the drafting tools inside Word. Arrows created against a picture in Word using the Word tools do not associate completely with the picture. Thus if you have to reformat the document for any reason, the pictures will move because they're embedded in line with the text, but the Word created arrows may or may not move correctly. The best way to create arrows in your picture is to do it using a photo manipulation tool. Paint Shop Pro, FastStone or Photoshop Elements will all do this. The arrows then become an integral part of the JPEG which you then embed as a single integrated image into the Word document. Thus the arrows move with the pictures, not independently.

If you're doing screen captures of your computer screen display, as I am in this book, it's best to paste the screen capture into a new JPEG file using your graphics tool. You can then manipulate the JPEG files in FastStone to set sizes and dpi's as required. FastStone has a screen capture tool built in under the File menu, which captures screen shots at 120 dpi and outputs them to a jpeg file, so that would be a preferable capture tool to the standalone products which produce lower dpi images. FastStone is my preferred tool and I use it heavily. It is also free to users, with a request to contribute if you find it a useful tool. Very strongly recommended if you're working with images.

While your book text should be 'fully justified', (justified to both left and right margins), when I have pictures on a page I set the pictures to 'center justified'. This places the pictures evenly on the page, where left, right or fully justified can leave them uneven on the page. I also set the paragraph setting to have no indent on the first line, so that the centering is truly centered.

We do need to discuss images, photographs and screen shots in relationship to eBook formats. In paper books, like CreateSpace, images should be submitted in at least 300 dpi, preferably higher. I usually submit at 350 or 400 dpi. These print out on paper cleanly and crisply. In eBooks, all images are reduced to 96 dpi, sometimes less. This is because the earlier eBook device screens couldn't deal with higher resolutions and the larger file sizes simply took up bandwidth during the download of the eBook. Technology has changed since those beginnings and screens are getting much better, especially the tablets being delivered today, with even higher screen resolutions to come. Trouble is, the eBook readers are still displaying images at 96 dpi, and the eBook creator software, including both Kindle and Smashwords, still generate eBooks with images downgraded to no more than 96 dpi. Both Smashwords and Kindle compress all images down to 96 dpi during the document preparation stage. For example, a 500 KB image will be reduced to 25 KB when doing the 'save as html' step when preparing the document for Kindle. The Word picture tool 'Compress' to 96 dpi does the same thing.

This isn't too much of a problem with photographs, as the human eye is very good at interpolating the image from just a few pixels. The small image of a photograph displayed on eBook readers looks small, but reasonable well defined. Only a few readers allow you to zoom in on the image, but when you do, you immediately see that the image is actually very granular and pixelated. The trouble begins when you use images which contain text, or other small but crucial details. There are simply not enough pixels shown in a single text character displayed at 96 dpi to be clearly seen on a small image. Enlarging the image simply magnifies the pixilation. This means that screen shots showing text will appear to be poor resolution in any eBook format or reader. There doesn't appear to be any way around the problem, until the eBook producers upgrade the level of image resolution they produce, and eBook readers display images at a higher resolution. This means that any image showing text or small details, and especially screen shots of textual displays, may look clean and crisp on the paper version of your book but will be pixelated and grainy in your eBook versions. Your choice then becomes, 'do I use it and accept the poor resolution, or do I scrap the image entirely?'.

For this book I have chosen to use the screen shots, even though the pixilation does detract somewhat from the eBook displays. I'm intending the screen displays as guides for you to follow along with, using the actual web site. The accompanying text provides the details that the screen shot cannot. I've adjusted the shots as much as I can to give a reasonably viewable image and hope that they're clear enough for you to follow. My apologies for the 'poor' readability of the text in the screen shots, but it seems to be unavoidable.

With photographs, the original image is at low dpi but comparatively large and can thus have the dpi increased by reducing the image size, without introducing artifacts, noise or pixilation into the picture. The size of the picture simply gets smaller as dpi goes up. Images like screen shots start out small and at low dpi, and it's simply impossible to increase the dpi while maintaining the size of the image. You would have to create detail where there is none in order to increase the dpi, and that does nothing more than create artifacts and noise in the image. The dpi goes up, but there is no additional detail, simply more grey, fuzzy dots in the picture. So, do the best you can with images in eBooks, but don't expect them to be of the same quality and crispness as the images printed in the paper version of your book.

In my how-to books I created a file folder for all the pictures used in the book, and then created sub-folders for source pictures, and for manipulated pictures. Thus I end up with all the pictures for each chapter in two file folders. For example, I use: ('bookname/pictures/chapter1/source/' and 'bookname/pictures/chapter1/forthebook/'). This makes it much easier to add new pictures or re-manipulate and re-import pictures into my Word document as and when required.

Some books now include a DVD of videos related to the book. This is impossible to do using any of the three publishing techniques I'm discussing, but there is a relatively easy way to provide videos to your readers. In my how-to books, in certain locations, I have added a web address which links to a video. That link points to a location on my own web site and connects viewers to an on-line video file. This allows me to provide several still photographs of the function I'm demonstrating in the book, and also allows me to provide access for the reader to on-line videos that they can view for more detail.

The video links on my website are 'unpublished', so you have to purchase the book in order to receive the web links providing access to those videos. By unpublished I mean there are no links on my homepage to those videos, nor are they published or promoted anywhere except in the book. They can only be accessed if you know the exact address. Thus a purchaser of the book can access the videos while those who don't purchase the book cannot, or at least they can't find them very readily. This is a fairly low tech approach, and not particularly secure as web crawlers and search engines can still find the files, but it's not wide open like a YouTube video and it provides sufficient security for my purposes. You can post your videos on YouTube if you want, but then they're accessible to anyone, even those who haven't purchased your book. For my third 'how-to' book, Advanced Soapstone Techniques, I posted the videos on YouTube to see if they would act as an advertisement for the book. At this point I don't think they did, but they did provoke some comments from viewers, who may have purchased the book later. Time may tell, and in the meantime, I'm treating those videos as a sales tool.

I shoot the original videos in HD 1080p format to get the highest resolution and maximum video quality and then allow the Google or YouTube website tools to convert to its preferred format during the upload to the website. I'm looking at converting the videos to Flash Player files, but for now they're in Windows Media format. As with the photographs, I keep videos in chapter related folders in order to easily keep track of where they are and how they relate to the book.

We'll discuss setting up the web pages in a later chapter.

Conclusions:

- take many photos and bracket the exposure of the photos
- test photo variations to get the best result
- keep the photos bright and clean i.e. white background and lots of light
- download the FastStone software and get to know it
- keep your photos well organized, with backups
- resize all pictures to at least 350 dpi for inclusion in your book
- if you use screen shots, make the original screen capture as large as you can
- make videos available via your website with links embedded in the book text, or upload them to YouTube

Technical Complexity: low to medium

Should be fairly familiar with digital cameras, setting exposure and bracketing, lighting, use of flash, photo manipulation tools, dpi adjustment, color adjustment.

For videos and web links, complexity is medium and requires familiarity with tools such as Google and / or YouTube web tools and video uploading.

Note: managing and using photographs is obviously not required for text only books.

Headers, Footers and Sections

The next step in making your text ready for paper publishing is to add in page formatting, paragraph styles, headers, footers and page numbers. If you've been adding text to a downloaded CreateSpace Word template, then your document should already be sized and formatted as required.

However, adding to the template doesn't always work properly, so I sometimes do a manual format when I'm pretty sure I am done adding partial files to my master document. When I say doesn't work properly I mean you've done a 'cut and paste' rather than a 'cut and paste special', and thus inadvertently brought in extraneous formatting information.

In Word, open your master document. From the menu, click on the Edit, Select All option. Then go to File, Page Setup and set the options as required, as outlined earlier in the chapter 'Building Your Paper Book'. Alternatively you can open the CreateSpace template and look at the settings there and then transfer those same settings to your own document.

Next, with the entire document still selected, go to Format, Paragraph and set your preferred paragraph options; indents or no indents, trailing spaces, justification, etc. Then go to Format, Font and set the font type and size. This will reformat your entire document to those settings.

This may cause a few issues which you will have to go back and fix. If you have photos in the text, you'll need to find them and set them to no indent, centered or to your own preferred style. If you've decided to leave them in the base style then this step is not required.

If you used more than one font, ie. Bookman for text and Verdana for titles and chapters, you'll now have to re-set them where required.

Using the template avoids all this extra work, but you need to make sure that none of your file imports via the 'cut and paste' process has introduced alternate settings. If you always import using the 'Paste Special, Unformatted Text' option then the pasted text will always take on the properties from the template. If you simply 'Paste', the import will bring in the formats used on the original document, and thus will introduce unwanted changes to font, size, paragraph styles, indents, etc.

Once you're happy with the basic style, size and formatting of your document, you're ready to tackle headers, footers and page numbers.

In order to do this properly we need to also introduce Word 'Section' breaks. To make things easier, all your text should be finished, edited, formatted and page setup completed before you start working with sections, headers and footers.

In order to properly assign headers, footers and page numbers, we need to break the book up into Sections. The first section is the **front matter:** the title page, copyright page, dedication, disclaimer and preface. The table of contents can be included in the front matter or it can be in its own section. If you have a prologue it can be included in the same section as the table of contents, or can also be it's own section. The body of the text becomes it's own section, and anything after the body, referred to as the **back matter,** becomes the final section. The back matter includes things like indexes, glossaries, appendices and bibliography.

You create sections in Word by using the 'Insert, Break, Section Break', menu options. I prefer to use the 'Section Break, Next Page' and then control insertion of any required blank pages myself. Set your cursor at the position in your document where you want a break to occur and then insert the section break. When you're working with Word's Section Breaks, there are several options; 'Continuous, Next Page, Odd Page and Even Page'. Continuous means put in a section break but don't do anything else. Next page means insert a section break and skip to the top of the next page. This is the equivalent of a simple 'Page Break' but also adds a section break. Odd and even mean insert a section break and skip to the next odd or even page in the Word document, respectively. I don't like them because they can insert 'invisible' blank pages, not evident in the Word display, but showing up when you print to PDF format. This can throw off your book interior pagination. What Word considers to be odd and even pages does not necessarily match up to what the book printing tools thinks are odd and even pages.

Section breaks are required because they allow you to adjust headers, footers and page numbers specifically by section. Adjusting headers and footers within and across section breaks does take a little getting used to. It's not uncommon to set a header or a footer inside a section, go to a different section and set a different header or footer, and find your second change has just overwritten the first change. The key to preventing this overwriting of changes is to make sure you disable the 'Link to Previous' option in the header / footer menu. When enabled, this option means the header or footer in section 5 is inherited from the header or footer of section 4. You don't want inheritance between front matter, body text and back matter, because you will want different headers and footers in those sections. However, within the body of the text, you will use the inheritance feature to make your own life easier. When working with sections, headers and footers, it's best to start at the beginning of your book. Don't start in the middle, as that will really confuse things.

By default, Word automatically makes your entire base document Section 1. Once we start adding additional section breaks, the front matter section will become Section 1. Place your cursor immediately before the start of the body of your text, which is usually at the beginning of the first chapter heading. Insert a Section Break, Next Page. Then go to chapter 2 and repeat the process. Work through the entire book, making each chapter its own section, with the section break immediately before the chapter heading. This will make the chapter page the 'First Page' of your headers, and that's exactly what we want. Once you've got all the section breaks in place we will start adding headers and footers.

Within a book, it's considered to be bad form to have headers appearing on pages where a new chapter begins. Don't ask why, but it is. Look at a few books with chapter breaks. In professionally printed books there won't be a heading on those pages. So how do we do that without using some sort of fancy and expensive page layout software. Easy!

Word provides you with three types of headers and footers within a section. The 'First Page' header, the 'Odd Page' header and the 'Even Page' header. The key here is the First Page header.

For Section 1, the front matter, we don't want any of the pages to have any headers, footers or page numbers. Put the cursor at the beginning of Section 1, select 'View, Headers and Footers' from the Word menu bar and set all three types, First, Odd and Even, to blank.

Next, place the cursor on the first page of Section 2, which should be Chapter 1. Set the 'First Page Header' to blank and the First Page Footer to have the page number only. Set the page numbering to start at page 1. Now set the Even and Odd page headers to contain your chosen header material, and the footers to contain the page number. For my headers, I put the author name on one page and the book title on the other. I prefer the author on the left page of the book, and title on the right, but the reverse is just as acceptable. It should look like this:

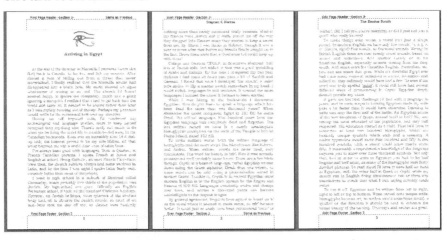

Now, at the next chapter page, you've already inserted a Break, Section, Next Page, so place the cursor on the first page of this section, in this case it will be Section 3. This will automatically make the first page of the chapter the first page of the section, which should default to 'same as previous'.

Thus the first page of each chapter / section will inherit the previous sections first page headers and footers. Format the page number in the footer to 'continue from previous'. Now set the Even and Odd page headers and footers to be 'same as previous' so Section 3 inherits the information from Section 2. The remainder of the chapter pages will contain the appropriate header and footer content. Continue to go through the book adjusting the headers and footers at the beginning of each chapter / section. This will automatically remove the header from the first page of each new chapter. Your headers and footers are now formatted to professional standards. Scan through your book and make sure everything is correct, chapter pages with no headers, other pages with headers and all page numbers are properly sequential.

To see the section break inside the text, click the Show Hide button on the Word menu bar, the one that looks like ' ¶ '. This will show spaces, paragraph endings, tabs, page breaks and section breaks. Section and page breaks will show as lines across the page. An example section break is shown below.

================Section break (Next Page)===================

Now go through your book inserting page breaks, section breaks, headers and footers wherever you feel appropriate. The simplest book will have three sections, the front matter, the body text, and the back matter. The back matter section may consist of no more than a blank page, but you still don't want headers, footers or page numbers to appear on the blank page, so set those headers to blanks. Notice that Word's status bar, usually displayed at the bottom left of your screen, shows the page you're on, the section the cursor is in, the current page number and the total number of pages in the book. This is one way of telling which section you're in.

As mentioned, be a little wary of section breaks. I've often found on review that the Word document looks as if it's done the page breaks correctly, but when I print to PDF format I find extra pages where I didn't intend them, usually caused by inserting an *odd* or *even* section break. Word's print preview will show these hidden blank pages but I always print to a PDF file to check my final page break pattern.

Your book page numbering should always start with the page on the right hand side of the book and page one should always be the first page of your text body. Open any book, and the title is on the right hand page. Trouble is, in Word, the first page is always on the left of a two page display. It does make page numbering and page break alignments a little interesting when you first start, because what Word considers to be an odd page, the final print format considers an even page, and vice versa. The solution is to print to PDF and check, and then double-check again when you get to the on-line Reviewer tool CreateSpace provides. The CreateSpace tool will always be the final decider, because what it displays is exactly the way the book will appear in print.

On the 'first page footer' of section 2 (which is Chapter 1, page 1), when you create the page number it will default to the actual page number of the manuscript, anywhere from 6 to 12 depending on how many pages are in your front matter. You want this to start at number one, so within the header / footer panel, select the button to 'Format Page Number' and set the starting number to 1. If you have a section before the body of the text but after the front matter, say a prologue, and you want that to have page numbering in the Roman style, i.e. 'i, ii, iii', this can be done from the same 'Format Page Number' option. On the first page header of section 2, the text body, you do not want any header. The very first page of the book text, usually the introduction, normally has only a page number at the bottom. Headers don't normally start until the second page of the body of the text. Remember the first page of text in your book is always the odd page, page number 1, and is on the right hand side of the book.

When you've added text to the header or footer I recommend that you select the text and then set the font color to either 80% or 50% gray. This reduced gray level makes the headers and page numbers less intrusive to the reader. I also make the header text one or two points smaller than the font I used in the body of the book, and center them on the page. Using my standard, the body of the book is in Bookman Old Style

11 point, so my headers and footers will be in Bookman Old Style 9 point, 80% gray in color and centered.

That's my personal preference but again you can use your own standards. Some books put the author name left justified and the book title right justified, or vice versa. The page number is almost always at the bottom of the page, but can be left, right or center justified. Some books put the author and book title on the bottom along with the page number but that's pretty unusual and it tends to look a little crowded.

An alternative option is to put the author name on one page and the <u>chapter</u> title on the other, replacing the name of the book. If you choose to do this you will have to modify the header and footer of every chapter / section. This makes for a lot more work and should definitely be left until the very last thing you do to your book, as any change in chapter sequence would require an equivalent amount of work changing the section header sequences.

The final section is the rear matter. This section may be simply a blank page to end the book. For example, if your text ended half way down a right handed page, the back of the last page will be blank. It looks much more professional for blank pages to be blank, without any header, footer or page numbers.

If the back matter includes appendices or bibliographies, you may or may not want them to have headers, footers or page numbers. Thus they may all be in a single section, or you can break the back matter into multiple sections with differing headers and footers.

For this book, I have an Appendix and a 'Notes from the Author' page in the back matter. I've formatted these so that they both appear on the right hand page of the book, so there is a blank page between them. To do that I made the Appendix one section and the Notes page a second section. The single blank page between them becomes the 'First' page. I then edited the headers and footers of the 'First page' of each section to display no headers or footers, and set the 'odd' page headings of each section to inherit from the previous section. This puts my standard headers and footers on the 'odd' page' of each section, while the intervening blank pages have nothing on them.

Once you think you're finished setting up all the sections, headers and footers, you should always do a full review of your document to ensure that all of your headers and footers are where they are supposed to be and display exactly what you want displayed. After making changes to headers and footers it's not unusual to find that something has bled over between sections and you now have a footer or header where you don't want one.

Once you're sure you're finished, print the document out to a PDF file, review it on screen. Make sure all your page and section breaks are where you want, that all the headers and footers are where you intended them to be, all the blank headers and footers are correctly placed, and all your page numbers are in place and sequenced correctly.

Doing things like this does require more work, more fiddling around to get things exactly the way I want them, but that's one of the beauties of self publishing. I can make things exactly the way I want them, with no publishing house editor telling me how I must do it.

Technical Complexity: medium

Should have familiarity with Word headers, footers, page numbering, section and page breaks, font formatting and text alignment.

Table of Contents and Chapter Headings

Your book is almost ready. You've written the internal text, built the title page, the copyright page, dedication and the disclaimer. The font has been selected and set throughout the document, as have the line spacing, paragraph style, indenting, sections, headers, footers and page numbering. There's just a few more things to do.

Every book is broken down into chapters. Some books have a Table of Contents, some don't. I always build a Table of Contents while I'm writing the book, even if I intend to delete it before I publish, as I do for novels. This provides me with a single page reference for all of the contents of my book in the sequence in which they appear. This is very important as you may want to vary your chapter sequence so as to make the text flow more smoothly. This applies even to novels and memoirs.

Word provides a simple way of doing this. Highlight your chapter heading and change the style to Heading 1, 2 or 3. The style 'Heading' allows Word to generate a Table of Contents quickly and easily. The Style box is on the upper left corner in Word 2003, and will usually show the word 'normal', meaning normal text style, or 'body text'. I use Heading 3 for my Chapter Headings, as the other headings use much larger font sizes, and I have no real use for three levels of heading. I have also modified the style of Heading 3. If you want to you can go into Word's style manager and change the heading style to suit your own requirements.

My heading style is Monotype Corsiva, 18 point, bold, center justified, with 65 point spacing before the title and 25 point spacing after the title. This spacing, set using the 'Format, Paragraph' tool, while inside the Style Manager, brings the chapter heading down from the top of the page, and pushes the text down from the heading, thus making a chapter title more distinct and recognizable. All of these items can be adjusted in Word using the Style Manager. Click on the down arrow of the style selection box, scroll down to the bottom of the list and select the 'more..' option. A box will appear on the right side of the Word window. You can now select any style used in the document and modify it to meet your own requirements.

Once all your chapter headings have been changed to style 'Heading 1, 2 or 3' you can build your table of contents. Place the cursor in the location of your document that you want the Table of Contents to appear in. From the Word menu bar, go to 'Insert, Reference, Table of Contents', select the level and style you want and click OK. The Table of Contents will be built, including page numbers if that option box is ticked.

The Table of Contents usually appears before the first chapter or prologue, but after the rest of the front matter. If you intend to keep the table in your printed book, you may also want to make the table it's own section, so you can control headers and footers independently of the rest of the book.

If you are using a Table of Contents, Word's automatic creation tool is quite adequate for production of the paper version.

I create a table of contents for all my books while I'm writing them, as a cross reference tool so I can easily see how the chapters sequence. It also shows if I've made a mistake on my sections, as the page numbers will be out of sequence. For those books which don't require a table of contents in the final print, such as a novel, I simply remove the table just before finalizing the document ready for printing.

EBooks require a slight modification to this process for generating a Table of Contents that eBook readers can use, and we'll cover that when we get to creating the eBook master document.

Technical Complexity: low to medium

Should have familiarity with Word styles, style editing, paragraph formatting, table of contents.

Document Review and PDF Creation

At this point your book text is finished. Your front matter section is complete, the body of your text is properly formatted, spell checked, reviewed and edited, section breaks and page numbers are correct, headers and footers are correct, your bibliography is complete and your final Table of Contents updated.

Now review your entire document on-screen. I do this in several ways. First, run Word's spell checker. Make sure you're using the correct language and spell dictionary: UK English versus Canadian English versus US English versus whatever language you're writing in. Correct any mis-spellings. I don't use Word's grammar checker as I find I disagree with most of its recommendations. Again, that's a personal choice. Feel free to use the grammar checker if you want.

Next, set Word's zoom factor to around twenty percent. That's too small to see the text, but you can scan the pages in their entirety and quickly spot anything that looks odd. This includes things like a page that has an odd or uneven layout, extra gaps between paragraphs, blank pages and photo pages which look lopsided because the justification is wrong.

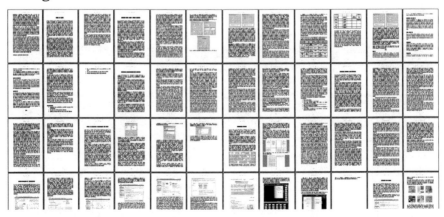

My default paragraph for novels includes a 0.25 indent. However, if I have pictures inserted in the document, the indent causes them to be off-set, so I need to set my paragraph indent to none for all pictures. This is most easily done by using the twenty percent zoom view, as I can set my paragraph indent for the first picture, and then quickly move through the document, selecting pictures and pressing CTRL Y to repeat the last format command.

Next, set the zoom factor so that you have four pages displayed side by side. I'm using a twenty seven inch monitor, set to 1920 x 1080 screen resolution, so for my setup the zoom factor is forty percent. That will be different for you depending on your own screen size and resolution setting. In Word's zoom box, simply type in the zoom factor you want, or select one of the pre-defined factors. Skim through your entire document again, looking at the way the text flows across the page. Properly formatted text should look neat and tidy and have some symmetry to it. Investigate anything that looks odd or different.

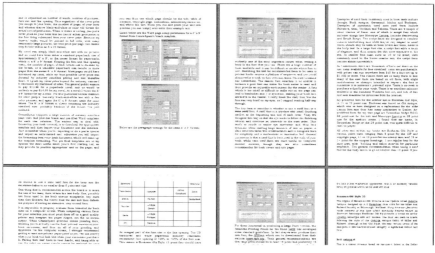

Now set the zoom to get a two page side by side display. In my case that's one hundred percent. You should be able to read the text comfortably at this point. If not, set the display so the text is easily readable. On smaller displays this may mean going to a single page display.

Now, read the entire book, carefully, as if for the very first time. Focus on seeing the words written, not reading what you intended to write. You're doing a final edit check, looking for poor sentence structure, bad grammar, words that are spelt correctly but used in the wrong place, such as 'there' vs. 'their', words that are missing, etc. You should also review the overall flow of the information or story. Does the sequencing make sense and flow smoothly, or is it disjointed? If it doesn't flow nicely, think about re-sequencing the content or the chapters. On my first book I ended up moving several chapters around, making the story line flow more smoothly from one event on to the next. You may need to redo this step a few times to double check that your changes haven't introduced new errors. Once you're happy, you should get a couple of other people to read the book, checking for the same issues. Keep re-reading and re-editing until you're satisfied the book is ready for publication. Once you're happy with your final version you need to print your document to PDF for submission to CreateSpace.

There are several PDF creation tools on the market, the most obvious one being Adobe's Acrobat Writer Pro. For our purposes the Acrobat Writer does a lot more than what we need, plus it's fairly expensive. I have found several free tools available which do a very nice job of creating PDFs and more than meet our quality requirements. These include, Bullzip PDF Writer, CutePDF Writer and PDFill PDF Writer. If you already own Acrobat Writer then by all means use it. CreateSpace provides a Help page defining the setup for creating an Acrobat optimized PDF for their conversion tool. If you don't own Acrobat, then I'd recommend BullZip PDF Writer as it seems to give a cleaner reproduction of the fonts inside the PDF file than the other free tools. Run Bullzip Writer after installation and set the 'Document' options to 'prepress' and the 'Image' resolution options to 720 dpi for both vertical and horizontal. The CreateSpace reviewer will give warnings if images are less than 300 dpi, and I've had no issues with either the Bullzip or Acrobat Writers. A PDF format file is the recommended file format to upload to CreateSpace's conversion tool for creation of the final printed book.

Every book requires a book cover, some type of picture or combination of picture and text which serves both to catch the eye and entice the reader. CreateSpace provides you with several options, which we'll cover in detail in the section on Book Cover Creation. It will be easier if you leave the actual creation of your cover until you've signed on to CreateSpace and reviewed their on-line options for cover creation, however there are some things to be aware of.

You can create a complete, combined front, spine and back cover and upload it, you can create separate front and back covers and upload them individually, or you can use one of the many default covers CreateSpace provides, a mix and match solution. Some of the provided covers allow you to upload your own pictures to fit inside frames on the cover while others provide the option of using pictures supplied by CreateSpace.

CreateSpace provides a good selection of front and back cover design layouts, offering different styles and themes. Styles control the layout of the cover, where the title goes and where the authors name goes, etc. Themes control the font types and sizes used for each piece of text. If you choose one of the preset covers you also have access to a variety of themes, colors and photographs provided by CreateSpace for your use.

If you choose to provide your own front and back covers created from scratch, you will need a graphics tool, such as Paint Shop Pro, Adobe Elements/Photoshop or possibly the open source graphics tool GIMP. I usually create my covers from scratch, using Paint Shop Pro. If you go this route, your first task is to find a first class, high quality picture for the front cover. This picture can come from your own photo archives, from a picture you took during the creation of the book while you were taking photos for interiors, or you can acquire photos from other places including the Internet. Just remember that if you use photos which are not your own you must also make sure you acquire the right to use those photos for commercial purpose, or get them from a site which clearly identifies them as free to use.

You will use text in your cover pages, both back and front, so make sure the color of your text contrasts cleanly and pleasingly with the background photograph or picture. Pale yellow lettering on a pale blue background will be unreadable, so chose wisely. You must also keep in mind that this picture will probably be used for both the cover of your paper book and also for the thumbnail display for the eBooks and web pages, so text should be clear and easy to read.

The ability to carefully review your front and back covers is another reason you should always get at least one paper proof copy of your book. The online review tools are excellent but you simply cannot beat holding the book in your hand and seeing the detail of the photos, the text, layout etc. for yourself.

Once you have created your front and back covers and you're satisfied with the way they look when reviewed using the online tools, you should also create a versions of the front cover for the eBooks. I usually create a picture which is 2,500 x 1,666 pixels at 200 dpi for my eBook front cover. This size and detail format can then be used for both Smashwords and Kindle eBook covers. That level of quality and detail provides good visibility when displayed as a thumbnail on the webpages. Small enough to fit neatly on the page while being large enough for the reader to see both the picture and title text on the picture.

Your back cover usually has a 'blurb' on it, where a blurb is a brief description of your book. Basically a short description or advertisement as to why the reader, having picked your book out of the web lineup, or off the bookshelf in the store, should bother to purchase the book. All three of the publishing companies that we use here will accept both a short description and a long description of your book, making it available on their websites alongside your book title. Thus you should prepare at least two and possibly three blurbs for your book.

The size of the blurbs are based on the number of characters allowed. The long blurb can be up to 4,000 characters long. The short blurb can be no more than 400 characters long. These counts both include spaces between words and blank lines between paragraphs. Both should be written carefully and reflect the key points or issues that your book addresses and be written so as to entice the reader to purchase your book. Compressing your book, which may be in the order of 80,000 or more words long, to 4,000 characters is hard but not impossibly so. Compressing the same book into 400 characters can be almost harder than writing the book itself. It's not unusual to end up with ten or twenty drafts and reviews of the two blurbs. Usually, you can use a subset of the 400 character blurb on the back cover of your book. If this is not appropriate, or makes the text on the cover too small, then you will also have to write a shorter blurb to go on the back cover.

I recommend writing the 4,000 character blurb first, then the 400 character one, and then the one for the back cover of your book. Store the blurbs as separate Word documents. You will use these documents as sources for cutting and pasting into the various web fields on the publishing sites. I usually name them, very creatively, '4000 char blurb', '400 char blurb', 'back cover blurb', and store them in a folder called blurbs. Use Words 'File, Properties, Statistics' to see the character counts of each file.

You should now have your book text, front and back covers and two or three blurbs. You're ready to upload your files to CreateSpace and begin the process to publish your book in soft cover.

It's easiest if you have all your files, ISBN codes, covers and blurbs ready for upload before you start the process, though it's not mandatory, as you can upload the pieces in almost any order. However, some of the CreateSpace workflow requires you to have some things done before others, so you may as well have the files ready, with some exceptions. For example, the spine width for the cover cannot be calculated until after you've uploaded the book interior, as it is based on the number of pages there are in the book. If you're using CreateSpace generated covers then you need to upload the document before you begin the cover, so you won't have the cover files ready until after you've started the publishing process.

Technical Complexity: low

Should be familiar with Word, zoom, spell and grammar checkers, be able to download and install software packages, print to specifically selected printers for pdf creation.

Upload to CreateSpace

In order to upload files to CreateSpace you obviously need to sign on first. Go to www.CreateSpace.com and sign up to create an account for yourself. The expectation is that because this is your publishing site you will supply true and correct information about yourself. Name and address are especially important because that's who the cheque will be made out to. By all means review CreateSpace's privacy policy before doing so, but I've never had any issues with the site. Once your account is created sign in to CreateSpace. This will bring you to your member dashboard, which provides complete management of all your projects.

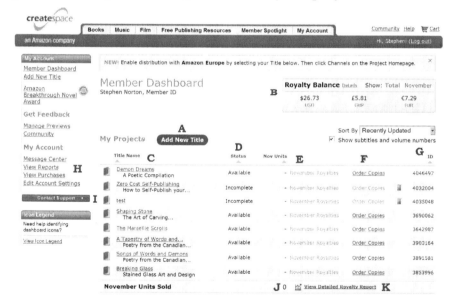

This is your CreateSpace homepage. **A** is to add a new title, **B** shows your current balances across all three markets, US, British and European. **C** lists the titles you currently have either completed or in progress. **D** shows the status of each title, 'Available' means people can buy it. **E** indicates the number of books that have been sold in the current month and that royalties were accumulated. **F** is the option to click on if you wish to order your own copies at the author wholesale price. **G** is the CreateSpace ID assigned to each project or book. Each book has a unique ID which is used both to track the book and to provide a marketing and sales page for that specific book. **H** is the menu to access other items, including messages from CreateSpace, your royalty reports, including customized reports you can build yourself, any purchases you have made and the options to edit your account settings. **I** gives you access to e-mail and telephone support, which in my experience is excellent. **J** is the number of books sold this month and **K** provides a detailed breakdown of how your books are selling. All activities are started from this page.

To add a new book simply click the 'Add New Title' button. This will bring up the new title creation page where you name your project and decide what the project is. CreateSpace allows you to create paper books, audio CDs, MP3s, DVDs and video downloads, all of which can then be distributed to sales sites.

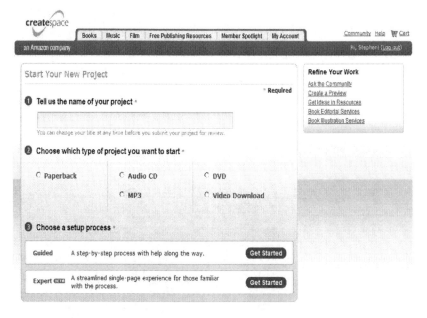

Select Paperback and provide a title for your project. I normally use my book title here. Next, select the method you wish to use in the setup process: guided or expert. For your first couple of books it's probably best to use the 'Guided' process. Once you're used to the workflow you can use the single page 'Expert' option which allows you to skip around from step to step.

The next step is the title information. If you named your project with the title of your book then the title is already filled out. Simply double check it for spelling and capitalization. I use 'cut and paste' from the Word Master copy of my book document for filling out a lot of the fields here. This ensures that the titles and subtitles I've used in the book are correctly replicated in the web pages. Complete the primary author field and if there are multiple authors use the 'Add Contributors' option. Enter the subtitle if you have one and then press the 'Save & Continue' button. This will save the project title information and take you on to the ISBN screen.

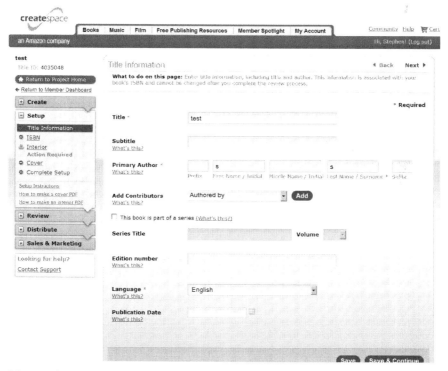

If you have an ISBN of your own that you wish to use select that option. If you do not have an ISBN and are only going to be publishing one or two books, then it's probably easiest simply to accept the free CreateSpace assigned ISBN. This does not affect your ownership of copyright to the book in any way. In order for the publishing companies to make your book available for sale on their web pages and other distribution outlets the book must have an ISBN. When done, click the 'Assign this ISBN' button.

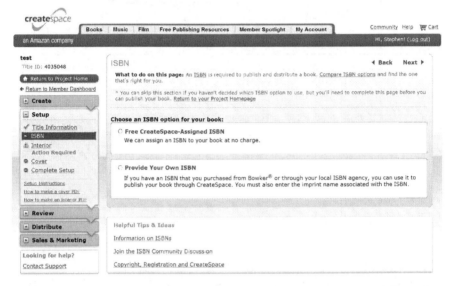

This will move us on to the interior page setup. At this point you can select the book trim size. Your first time through you will be asked to select the trim size. Later, if you do a second book, the previously selected trim size will be the default. Think of trim size as the size and shape of your book. Standard sizes offered range from 5" x 8" up to 8.5" x 11", with a variety of intermediate sizes. The 6" x 9" is a good standard size for novels, memoirs, etc. while larger sizes like 8" x 10" or 8.5" x 11" are preferably for 'how-to' books or books with a lot of color photographs or images. Go through your bookshelf or the library to get a feel for which book size would be the most appropriate for your book.

Next you must choose your interior type; black and white (for text only books) or full color (for books with color photos), and the paper color you wish to use, white or cream.

For novels with no pictures, black-and-white type and a page color of white are the usual choices. For memoirs which include photos or how-to books which include photos, the full color option may be the preferred option. If using full color, the cream paper option is greyed out. For my poetry books I used an interior type of black and white with cream paper color. This produces a book that is more aesthetically pleasing for poetry.

After selecting your typeface and paper color, you're ready to upload your book file. Note that if you selected the 6" x 9" option in CreateSpace, both your Word document and the PDF document you create from it must also use the 6" x 9" paper size option.

Click on the 'Browse' button and browse to the location on your PC where you stored the PDF version of your finished book. CreateSpace will accept a .doc or .docx Word document but providing a PDF ensures that the page layout remains exactly the way you set it. Supplying a .doc file can allow some variation to occur during the conversion. For example, I uploaded a .doc file and the print checker reported missing 'Vivaldi' fonts which needed to be embedded in my document. I didn't use Vivaldi anywhere in my document, but somewhere in the Word document defaults, Vivaldi must have been referenced. After I re-opened my Word document and produced a .pdf file, using BullZip, the 'erroneous' warning disappeared.

Once your file is selected you will be prompted to set the bleed, which should be the rightmost option, 'ends before the edge of the page' and whether or not you want to run the interior reviewer.

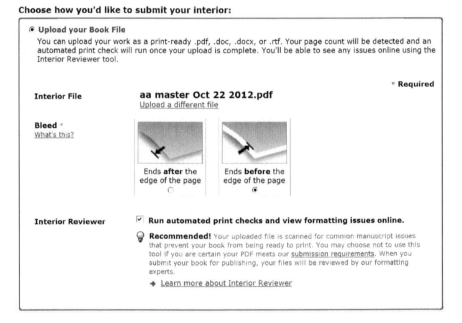

The interior reviewer allows you to review online what your document will look like after conversion. I recommended very strongly that you use it. Scroll down and click on the 'Save' button to begin the upload and conversion process. This will take a few minutes so be patient.

Note that there is a option shown on the webpage to talk to CreateSpace about professional interior design services, for a fee. CreateSpace provides professional assistance at all stages of the publication process, but if you're prepared to do it all yourself you can produce professional output. If you do it all yourself your production costs are zero. If you decide to use the offered services then obviously your production cost will not be zero.

The conversion can take several minutes but once it's done the webpage will warn you if any issues were found during the automated print check and give you the option to launch the reviewer. Launch the Interior Reviewer and review your document.

Automated Print Check   Cancel ☒

This will take just a few minutes.

We're checking your file for issues that affect how your book is printed. You'll be able to see any potential issues online using the Interior Reviewer tool.

Resolving potential issues now helps make the file review process go by more quickly.

🕐 Start working on your book cover while you wait.
We'll email you when your check is complete.

The print checker will scan for gross errors in formatting and photographs with a dot-per-inch resolution of less than 200 dpi. Low res pictures show grain and distortion when printed. It also checks for margin errors, where text overlaps the allowable print areas.

Even if the automated print check didn't find any issues, click on the button to 'Launch Interior Reviewer'. The interior reviewer acts like an book reader of your actual book, as it will look when printed. It allows you to review your document, either as a page by page display or as an overall view of all pages at once. As we did in our final step on preparing the Word document, review both the overall and the page by page displays, looking for any discrepancies or issues.

Because of the different display method, errors which may not have been visible in the Word or PDF versions can show up at this stage. Incorrect use of 'Section Break, odd or even page' are most easily seen here. Be aware that this is a more reliable display, as it replicates what the book will look like, exactly. The previous displays you've used, in both Word and PDF file formats, are only approximate displays of the final layout. If your book looked fine in the previous displays, but looks wrong in this display, this display should be taken as the more reliable.

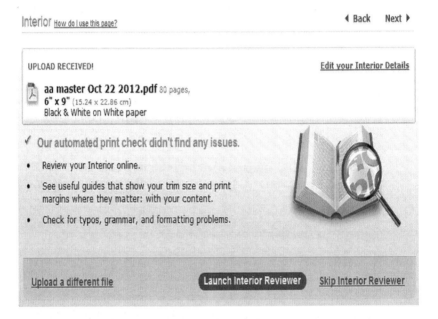

On the page by page displays there is a dashed box around the edge of each page. Anything extending beyond the dashed box is an error as this will not print correctly on the book. Return to your Word document and correct the margin issues.

Notice that the first page is displayed in 'real book' format, on the right-hand side of the book, exactly as if you had opened the book to the title page.

In the overall display (below), some of the pages have red stars beside them. This indicates that there is an error of some kind on that page. In some cases you may be prepared to accept the warning, for example, if the picture is less than two hundred dpi, but it's the only copy of the picture that you have. If the overall layout of your document meets your requirements, switch the reviewer to the side-by-side view again and check the book in detail.

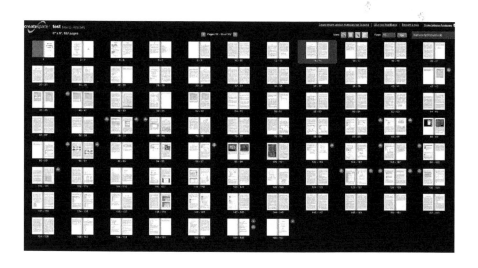

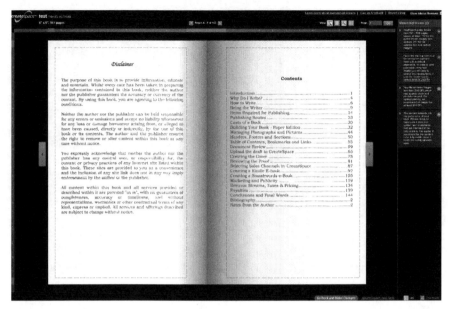

Review all pages which have error indicators, then go through the rest of the book looking for anything 'different'. This could be extra blank space where there shouldn't be any, titles that don't always fall the same distance down the page. In some books that may not be easily noticeable. In others, like my poetry books, where almost every page has a title, it's disconcerting to the reader to have titles bouncing up and down the page by a line or two. Make sure titles are always the same distance down the page. Careful use of style management and adding point spacing before and after the text on the chapter heading style should address this problem. Check that your selected fonts came through properly. If not, read up on Word's help files for embedding fonts in the document, or check the PDF writer to ensure it contains the fonts. If your selected fonts don't come through properly after two or three attempts, consider changing the font. Always check for spelling, correct word usage and grammar.

If you find any errors, like the margin issue below, now is the time to correct them. This display shows that my Bibliography page has it's margins set too far to the left, and thus some of my text will not be printed. This was probably caused by a 'Cut & Paste' which brought in formatting information from the separate Bibliography file. Repeat the paste using 'Paste Special, Unformatted Text' or simply adjust the margins on this one page in the Master Word document.

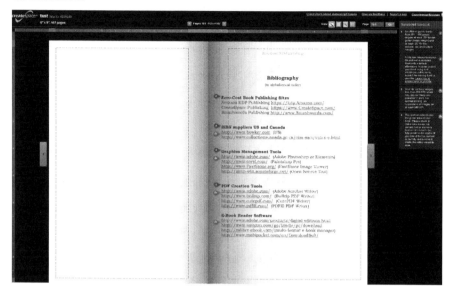

If any errors are found you must always go back to your Word document, fix the error, re-print to pdf and check on the pdf file. If everything looks good in pdf, re-upload the file to CreateSpace and then re-check with the On-line Reviewer tool.

Once you've completed your review and if you're happy with the book within the on-line reviewer, click on the 'Save & Continue' button. If you're not happy or found errors, go back to your original Word document and update it. If everything still looks good, then move on to the book cover.

Technical Complexity: low

Filling out web forms

Creating the Cover

From the Cover homepage you have three choices: build your own cover online, use CreateSpace's professional design group, for which there is a fee, or upload a print ready PDF cover you have created.

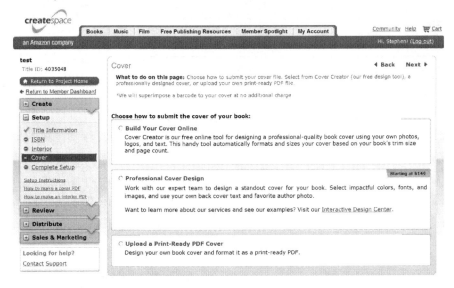

I found that uploading the print ready PDF cover is a bit painful because you have to manually calculate and adjust the book spine width depending on how many pages are in your book. This means if you've built your cover and then for some reason you add a section to the book, add more pages or remove a section, you must rebuild your PDF cover with a recalculated spine width. I've never used this method.

I've never used any of the professional services offered either, so can't provide any comments on the quality or usefulness of the services. However, our goal here is zero-cost, so we're going to do this step ourselves. I use the 'Build Your Cover Online' option, so let's select that option, and then go ahead and launch the cover creator.

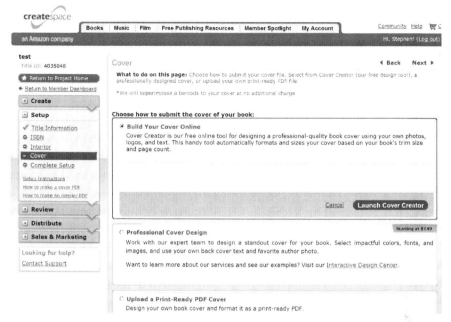

All cover designs are initially presented as 'Spineless'. This simply means that the template does not yet have a book spine width configured. This is done automatically by the system, based on the number of pages in the book.

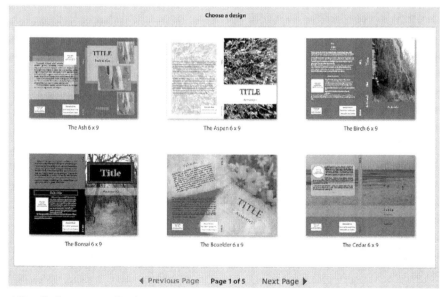

All of the supplied designs come with a default color scheme of matching background and font colors, but within the scheme you have some ability to change those colors. You also have the ability to use one of the default styles but still embed one of your own pictures into that style.

All the supplied options come with some areas blanked out, indicated by the white boxes in the examples above. These are reserved for things like the authors photo, your own publishing logo if you have provided your own ISBN, and a reserved space for the barcode which will go on the back cover. Barcodes are required in order to sell the book via most international booksellers. While you can choose to supply your own ISBN or use CreateSpace's ISBN, the barcode is always supplied by CreateSpace at no charge. Some of the possible cover designs are shown above and below. Note that not all covers have all the blank boxes. Some allow for only the barcode, some for the barcode and author photo and some for barcode, author photo and your own publishers logo. If you select a cover style with all three blanks, but only wish to use one or two, just leave that field blank. However, if you pick a style which does not have the blank you want, you can't add it in. In that case, you'd have to create your cover from scratch.

At this point you need to select a cover design. CreateSpace provides five pages worth of cover designs, so go through them carefully one by one and select the one that you like best. All of the options with pictures allow you to upload your own pictures. My preferred cover is the Palm on page 4 as it allows me to provide my own custom built front and back covers. This option adjusts the spine width appropriately as the number of pages in the book interior changes, so I don't have to worry about that.

For this book I'm going to start with The Elm, an option which doesn't have pictures. However because I selected this option doesn't mean I can't come back later, change my mind and select something else. Most of the fields that I complete for my first cover will carry over cleanly to another cover design. While I like the layout of the Elm, I'm not that enthusiastic about the orange default color so the first thing I'll do is change the color. Go ahead and select the cover design that you prefer. Within each design you have sub-options, called themes, which allow you to change the font styles, colors and background pictures. Different designs and theme combinations have different options, colors, fonts and text boxes, all of which you can modify to some extent. However, you do not have the ability to select the font of your choice from a large array of fonts, so a given design may be good, but you may not be able to get the font 'look' that you want.

The Mulberry 6 x 9

The Oak 6 x 9

The Pagoda 6 x 9

The Palm 6 x 9

The Pine 6 x 9

The Poplar 6 x 9

After doing some work on the Elm, changing colors, fonts and titles, I came to the conclusion that I couldn't make the Elm do what I wanted to do (mostly because of fonts and colors). So I switched back to my preferred standard, The Palm, which is the option that allows me to upload my own custom-designed front and back cover pages. However, because I do like the layout of the Elm cover, I'll replicate it in my graphics tool and simply use the fonts that I prefer. The main difference between the Palm and the Pine is the Pine expects you to upload the complete front, back and spine as a combined, single jpeg file, which means calculating your own spine width. I find it easier to simply use the Palm and let the system calculate the spine width for me.

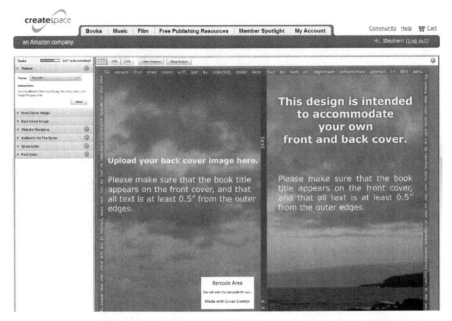

A full front cover for a 6" x 9" book should be a JPEG image file, 6.25" by 9.5" with a resolution of at least 400 dpi. I normally create my cover pages at 600 dpi. If you use other book sizes or book cover styles, be sure to check the CreateSpace instructions for the size that your cover page or partial page JPEG should be.

Using either of the options that require you to create your own cover from scratch does mean you need a graphics tool, something like Paint Shop Pro or Adobe Elements/Photoshop or the open source tool GIMP. If you don't have a tool like that and don't want to spend the money because you're only going to do one book, the easiest thing to do is use one of CreateSpace's provided title pages. Most still allow you to upload your own photo into the appropriate spot on the cover, or use one of the CreateSpace provided images. The free tool FastStone will allow you to do some image manipulation, like re-sizing, but is not really intended for full image creation. Any of these options enable you to create a professional looking cover without having to spend any money, nor do you need to spend a great deal of time and effort learning a graphics tool.

Obviously you won't create your CreateSpace book all in one sitting. You'll do a part and then come back later on to complete the next step. Simply clicking on the project title from your Dashboard will bring you to the overview page. This clearly indicates those areas that you've completed and those items which must still be dealt with.

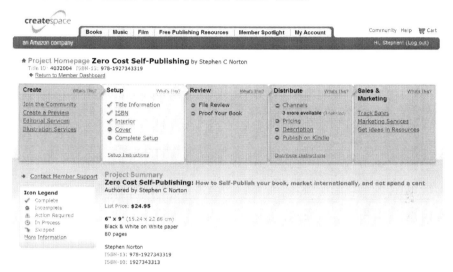

While the book is in progress I find it easier to use this page, as it provides me direct access to any stage of the publishing process. As you can see from the screen print above, I have completed the title, ISBN and interior steps, but my 'Cover' and 'Completing setup' have red icons beside them, indicating that those items are not yet completed. Selecting the 'Cover' option opens the 'Edit Cover' screen.

As I've already done some work on my cover I now have the option of continuing to edit my work to date, or starting over again using a different design. I'll continue editing. Note that the work I've done so far is displayed as a thumbnail image. It's worth noting that we can re-start our work at any stage, at any time during the publishing process, uploading a completely new interior file, re-starting the cover from scratch, selecting a different design, even changing the size of our book. You will get a warning that previous work will be lost, but you always have the option of beginning again if you're not satisfied with what you've done so far. This holds true across all three publishers we'll be using. You can always step back and re-start your project. The one exception is the ISBN. Once assigned to a book, the ISBN is permanently committed to that particular project.

Click on 'Edit Cover' to continue working on the cover. This will take you into the cover creation and edit screen.

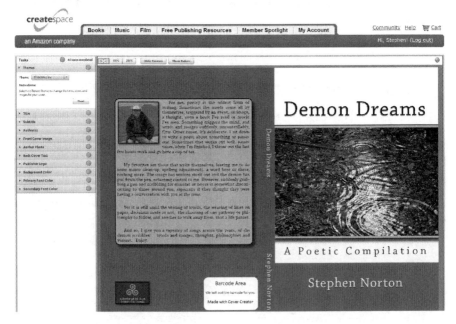

For my book 'Demon Dreams' I used a CreateSpace formatted cover and uploaded the picture from my own library. Notice that this pre-formatted cover has spaces reserved for Author Photo and Publisher Logo, and the back cover blurb is formatted inside a box. From the cover editor you can continue working on the cover until it's completed. Once finished, click on the 'Submit Cover' which will build the cover, create a thumbnail image and return you to the 'Edit Cover' screen. From there, click on the 'Complete Cover' button to submit the file for final processing.

Once all the steps are completed, and you've reviewed your interior and cover, completed all error corrections and are ready to call the book 'finished' select the option from the side menu to 'Complete Setup'. This will submit your completed files to CreateSpace for review.

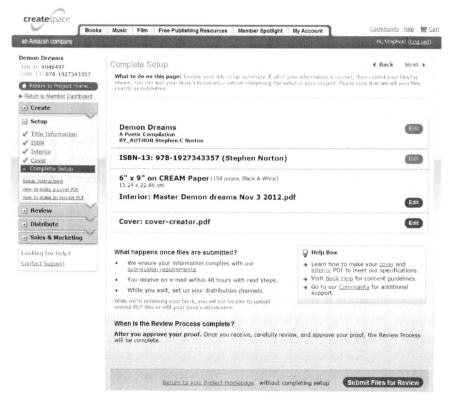

You'll get the message screen below and your book files will be frozen until after the review is completed. Your book isn't published yet, but we're getting close.

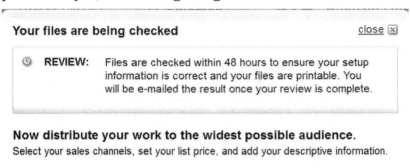

Once confirmed by CreateSpace, you will then be able to order a proof copy of your book and use the online proofing tools to review what your book will look like when printed.

You can still make changes after completing the setup, so if your 'Proof' has flaws you can submit a new interior file or re-edit your cover pages. You will be warned that changes may be lost on returning to the earlier screens but this means you'll have to re-submit files for re-build, so most of the work done on the cover page will still be there, you'll just have to repeat some steps on re-submission.

While you're waiting for the submission to be reviewed and approved, you can fill out the description fields of your book and set sales channels and pricing.

Technical Complexity: low to high

If using CreateSpace supplied cover designs complexity is low, mostly filling out web screen fields and uploading files.

If creating your own cover from scratch complexity can range from low to high, depending on the complexity of your graphic designs and your familiarity with the tools.

Selecting Sales Channels in CreateSpace

Select the 'Distribute' option from the Menu list on the left of the screen. This provides access to select the sales channels you wish to use, the price you want to assign to the book, create or modify your book description and optionally publish it as a Kindle eBook. Click on Channels to display the Channels screen. To select or de-select a channel, click on the arrow beside the channel name.

Notice that on this page there is a $25 option for expanded distribution. This is a CreateSpace option which gives you access to additional outlets. Below is an example of a book for which I did purchase the expanded distribution.

Within the no cost environment you have the option of the first three channels:

- Amazon.com (basically Amazon US)
- Amazon Europe
- CreateSpace eStore

You can pick all three or none of these. For example if you had written a memoir which you only wanted to distribute yourself and not make use of any of the web sales outlets whatsoever, you wouldn't select any of the channels. You would simply order books for your own consumption at the wholesale author price. If you're writing for the international market you would obviously pick all three. Note also that in order to access the library and other academic institutions you must use the ISBN number supplied by CreateSpace. You cannot use your own number. I have never made use of this option as I prefer to provide my own ISBN's.

Regardless of which sales channels you've selected, you need to set the retail cover price for the book. This is done through the pricing panel.

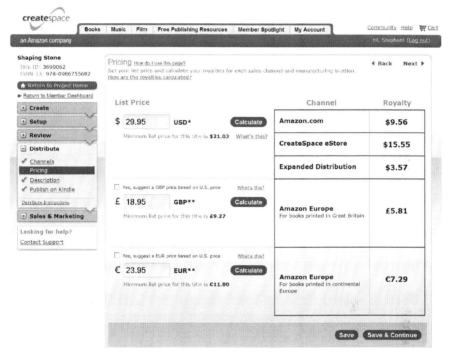

All pricing is set initially in US dollars and when you set the price the royalty field is automatically filled in for each of the other channels. If you selected Amazon Europe you also have the option to set prices for United Kingdom Pounds (£) and European Euros (€). To make your life easy CreateSpace automatically calculates those prices based on your US dollar price, however you can manually override those and set your own international pricing if you prefer. Notice that this book is one for which I purchased the expanded distribution and notice the royalty paid on the expanded distribution. As this book is aimed at zero cost publishing I will not comment on any optional packages which costs you money. Also notice the difference between the CreateSpace royalty and the Amazon royalty. Obviously it's preferable to sell your book directly from the CreateSpace web site, however Amazon has a much wider distribution outlet and is much more recognized among the general populace. Amazon may also offer a better shipping cost to purchasers than CreateSpace, a benefit to them, but a reduced royalty to you. Unless you wish to keep your book private and personal I would certainly recommend selecting all three of the free distribution outlets.

Next, click on the 'Description' option in the menu and fill out the description fields for your book by cutting and pasting from your 4,000 character blurb. This is critical for promoting your book as it's the only information the potential buyer will have to review your book, other than the cover image.

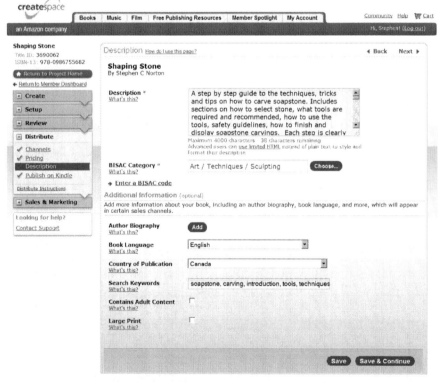

Then select the BISAC Category from the drop down menus. Spend some time here going through the various categories that may describe your book and pick the one that your book fits into the best. Some people browse for books by category, rather than searching by title or author name. Enter the language of the book, country of publication (your country, not CreateSpace's country) appropriate key words to support purchasers keyword searches and whether the book contains adult content or is in Large Print.

Once you've selected your sales channels and set your pricing the book is ready to be posted for sale, once you accept the proof of the book. CreateSpace provides a sale page for your book directly from CreateSpace, and if you selected the additional sales channels these web pages will become available within a few days, usually around 5 to 7 business days after you approve the book.

The CreateSpace web site for your book is the CreateSpace site address plus your book ID. For example the CreateSpace book sale page for my first novel, '**The Marseille Scrolls**' is:

http://www.CreateSpace.com/3642987

Amazon follows the same general format, and thus the book sale page for my book '**Breaking Glass, An Introduction to Stained Glass Art & Design**', on Amazon is:

http://www.amazon.com/dp/1927343089

The CreateSpace sales page is shown below, followed by the Amazon sales page.

Amazon also provides the author with an Author's Page where you can post your author picture, profile and biography and collect all your Amazon published books into a single location. This requires you to set up an Amazon account as well, which you will need to do when we get to creating the Kindle version of your book. We'll deal with the Amazon pages when we reach that point of publishing our book as a Kindle edition.

Breaking Glass Like 0

Stained Glass Art and Design
Authored by Stephen C Norton

Welcome to Breaking Glass, an introduction to the art and design of stained glass. A step by step guide to the techniques, tricks and tips on how to create Stained Glass Art, 'Breaking Glass' includes sections on selecting glass, the tools which are required and others which are recommended. Subjects covered include how to use those tools, safety guidelines, how to cut, grind, fit and assemble the pieces and display beautiful stained glass art. Each step is clearly explained via text, photographs and on-line videos.

Today, stained glass remains both an industry and a hobby. Churches still order stained glass windows for their cathedrals, mostly as depictions of scenes from the bible. Many commercial buildings have stained glass art prominently displayed. People buy stained glass 'Tiffany' style lamps for their living rooms and order colorful windows for their homes, ranging from scenery to abstract art. A good quality lamp can cost hundreds of dollars. Stained glass windows can easily go into the thousands.

As with any art, you can buy something created by someone else, or you can learn the art and do it yourself. Unlike some art forms, stained glass can be done in small scale by anyone with an interest and a steady hand. Pre-done patterns can be purchased at the local bookstore. Most cities have a glass shop which carries glass and stained glass supplies. If not, Internet sites abound. Tools are relatively inexpensive and easy to acquire. All you need is a little assistance, a guide to walk you through the steps of creation. What you have in your hands is that guide.

'Breaking Glass' is written to give you the introductory guide to creating stained glass art, including lampshades, windows and three dimensional objects. It introduces you to the various tools and techniques used, then walks you through the five steps of creating, cutting, grinding, assembly and finishing. Following along with the book allows the you to understand the art form, including creation of your own patterns. By the end, you will be able to tailor-make your own stained glass art.

I've chosen to make this book pictorial rather than wordy. I'm a firm believer that a picture speaks a thousand words, so I've tried to show, and only talked enough to guide you through what the picture depicts. I've also chosen the size of the book so I can fit in lots of pictures, while keeping the pictures big enough that you can clearly see the detail shown without needing a magnifying glass. At various key spots I also provide links to on-line videos, providing greater detail on techniques. Lastly, I've focused on giving you an overall introduction to creating stained glass art, so you can create your own designs and art to suit your needs.

You don't have to be an expert to follow the steps in this book. You don't have to have any experience in glass work, you simply need to have an interest and a desire to create something. I will guide you through the process in five easy-to-follow steps. You only need a few tools, though I show you other tools that can be useful. You can choose how much to invest and how many tools to buy. The basic tools can be purchased for one hundred to one hundred and fifty dollars. The glass is easy to buy and inexpensive, ranging anywhere from five to ten dollars per square foot.

Sound interesting? Well, if you haven't already done so, buy the book. Pick up a few tools, buy some glass, follow along with the book and let's start breaking glass.

List Price: $29.95

Add to Cart

Continue Shopping

Publication Date:	May 21 2012
ISBN/EAN13:	1927343089 / 9781927343081
Page Count:	114
Binding Type:	US Trade Paper
Trim Size:	8.5" x 11"
Language:	English
Color:	Full Color
Related Categories:	Crafts & Hobbies / Glass & Glassware

The CreateSpace page provides all the book information, size, color, number of pages, categories, etc, and displays the full 4,000 character description. Purchasers can be directed to this page and can purchase your book by adding it to the cart and supplying shipping and billing information. This page charges the full cover price you designated, so you, as the author, should not purchase copies for yourself from here. For buying your own copies, go to your dashboard and click on the 'Order Copies' option. The dashboard route will allow you to order copies for yourself at the manufacturers wholesale price.

If you've selected Amazon as one of your sales channels, CreateSpace passes the information on your book to Amazon for display on the Amazon Books webpage.

Notice that the Amazon web page also displays the 4,000 character description. On the Amazon page, clicking on the authors name will offer options to search for additional books by this author, or go to their author page.

We've completed all the ancillary information, and by now our book submission should have been reviewed, so let's go take a look at our 'proof' copy.

Technical Complexity: low

Filling out web forms

Reviewing the Proof

Once you have submitted your book to CreateSpace your files will be reviewed to ensure they meet CreateSpace's requirements. If they do, you'll receive an email stating:

> *Congratulations your files are printable!*
> *We've reviewed the interior and cover files for Your Book Title, #1234567 and they meet submission requirements.*
> *The next step in the publishing process is to proof your book:*

Now you can review the proof copy. As mentioned earlier, this can be done online, in which case there is no cost. However, as this is your first book, I do recommend spending the money to get a paper proof copy. Once you're familiar with the quality that CreateSpace produces, you can do it all on-line at no cost.

Ordering a single 'proof' copy of your book from CreateSpace is quite in-expensive. A 250 page black and white 6" x 9" book will cost less than $5.00, and shipping is reasonable: $6.99 to Canada, around $3.50 for most of the States. A full color book will cost more than a black and white book, but books are sold to the author 'at cost', so unless you have a 500 page full-color book the costs are quite reasonable. A 180 page 6" x 9" with full color photos every few pages costs $13.45. Having said that, definitely use the free on-line 'View a Digital Proof' tool <u>before</u> ordering a paper copy. You may find issues that you can correct before paying for the paper copy. Buying the paper copy at regular shipping rates also takes 2-3 weeks for delivery. Click on 'View a Digital proof'.

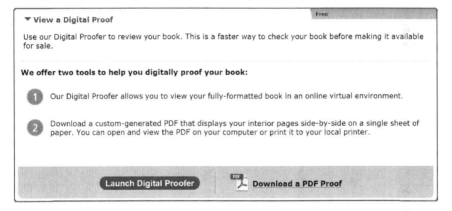

Like the online Reviewer tool, the online Digital Proofer tool is excellent, allowing you to view your book by full front and back cover, page by page and as a multipage display as shown below. It's basically the same tool as the Interior reviewer, but adds the cover pages to your review. You also have the option of downloading a PDF of your completed book. By all means do that as well, but I prefer to use the on-line tool as I believe it gives a more book-like view of the files. Click on 'Launch Digital Proofer' to review your book proof on-line.

The first screen displays the book's cover, back and front.

Check picture and text alignments of the covers, wording, make sure the text is easily readable and that there is no overlap on the reserved boxes such as the UPC code box.

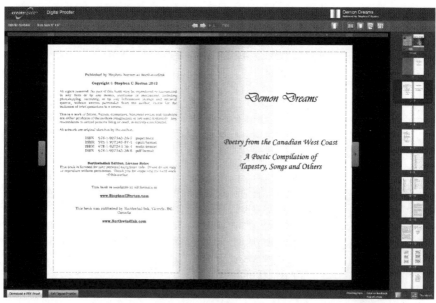

The next pages displayed are the first interior pages. As we did when we reviewed our book in Word and the interior reviewer, I recommend using both page by page and multipage displays. At this point I will check the first few pages, and then switch to the multi-page view.

The multipage display allows you to overview the book and see if any of your pages look odd or asymmetrical. This is very important for books such as the one displayed above where I have a lot of text wrapped around a lot of pictures.

Notice that on the example screen below, while there are no warning icons, I can easily see that the images are not all on the same side of the page. Remember the issues we had with section and page breaks in the Word document? The Digital Proofer allows you to double check the 'printed' version, to ensure that what you think is on the left page of your book, really is on the left side.

Here I can see that something has messed up my desired page layout. I wanted all the pictures on the left side of the book, but one of my section / page breaks was incorrect and some of the images ended up on the right hand side of the book. This should have been caught during the interior page review, but for whatever reason it wasn't. This means I must now go back to my original Word document, make adjustments, print to PDF, review the page layout and then upload the interior file to CreateSpace again. Uploading a new interior will force me to re-open my cover. In this case I simply need to open my cover for editing, then save the unchanged cover again. This forces the cover creator to re-calculate the spine width for the new interior, because my interior change may have changed the number of pages in the book. Now I need to re-submit all my files for review again, which will bring me back to this step, final proofing.

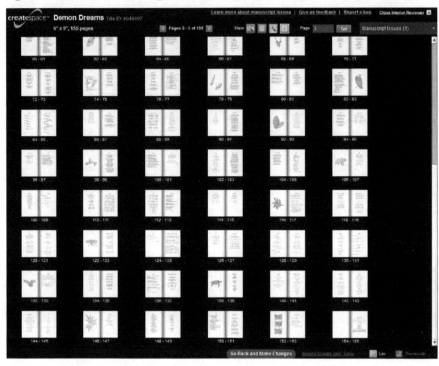

Even the book displayed below, an all text novel, benefits from the multipage review as you can see which pages look different from the others. Any differences or large blank spots should be investigated. While errors or oddities in page coverage should have been caught during the earlier interior review, it is not unusual to discover something you want to change even at this late date. Don't let it bother you if you find something you need or want to change. It's best to catch and correct things here, before you commit the book to being published and made available to readers. It seems that no matter how many times I edit check my books, every time I pick one up and read through it I see something I'd like to adjust, just to make it a little bit better. However, you do need to stop somewhere and actually print the book and release it for publishing and distribution.

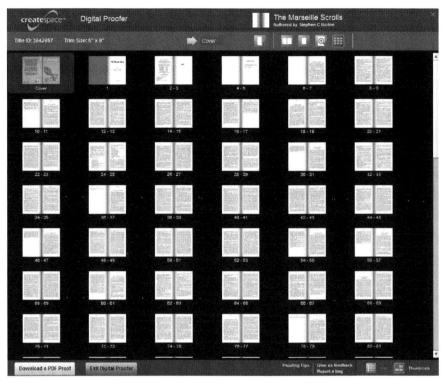

After any re-submission of your files, you should repeat the entire process of proofing your book. Check the cover again. Check the interior using the multi-page display again. Then select the page by page display for a detailed review of placement of text and pictures on each page.

Read through the entire book, page by page, checking for any errors. Are chapter headings aligned properly, is the text aligned on the page correctly, are headers and footers correct and on the right pages, are page numbers where you wanted them to be, on the right pages, and numbered sequentially and correctly? Again, check spelling and grammar, word use, etc. The online proofing tool provides an option to download a PDF of your finalized document and I recommend doing this and double checking things again.

Yes, you did all this on the Word document before you uploaded it, and you did it again on the interior reviewer after the upload. Now do it again. I know I've recommended double checking everything a lot of times, but it's very easy to overlook an error and the more times you check the more errors you will catch, and thus the more professional your end result will be. Murphy's Law says you will always find another thing to correct or change, no matter how many times you've checked before. There's nothing worse than getting your hands on the first copy of your just-released-for-sale book and immediately finding an obvious error on page four. My first novel had 'comment sa va' on page 1. I'd checked it on the on-line translators and they said it was fine, but the first three buyers all said it should have been 'comment ca va'. Turned out to be my Quebecois French (sa) versus Parisian French (ca), but everyone was much happier with 'comment ca va'. So I changed it and re-released the book as fast as I could.

Once you are finally satisfied that the document has been as proofed as you can possibly make it, go back into the Review screen and either order a paper proof, or click the button to 'Approve' the proof based on your digital review.

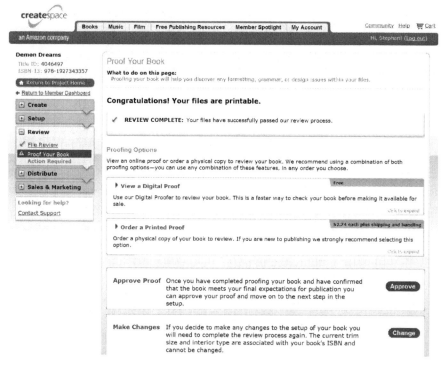

You'll be prompted one more time to confirm that you approve the book for publishing.

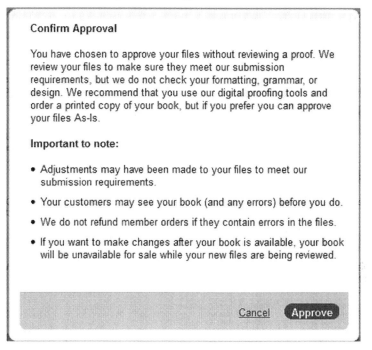

Go ahead and click on the Approve button to confirm that you approve the proof.

With the proof authorized, either from a paper copy or the online proofing tool, it becomes available for sale on the channels you have selected.

Your CreateSpace soft cover paper book is now complete. It's available for sale on CreateSpace, and will shortly be available for sale on the other sales channels you selected. Part one of three is complete, you now have the option of creating one or more electronic book formats of your book.

Smashwords creates .epub files and distributes to multiple vendor sites so let's create and publish an epub eBook next. However, before we can start that we need to do a little more work to our Master document.

close ⊠

Congratulations!

You've completed the setup of your book.

f Share your News

You can change your pricing, description information, and channels at any time in the **Distribute** section.

Your book will be available in the following timeframes:
Updates to your book will also appear in these timeframes.

- CreateSpace eStore: **Immediately**
- Amazon.com: **5-7 Business Days**
- Amazon Europe: **5-7 Business Days**

💡 **Want to market your work?**

➡ Learn how to get started in our Marketing Center

☑ Give us your feedback   **Close Window**

Technical Complexity: low

Filling out web forms and viewing web browser displays, reading and editing your paperback proof.

Creating an eBook Master

At this point we have a single Master document, formatted for use in creating a printed book. EBooks require some modifications to be made to that document, specific to e-Book conversion requirements. Pictures are a key issue, as eBooks are designed to have small file sizes, providing rapid download times and allowing many books to be stored on devices which have limited storage like Smartphones. Tables of Content are also an issue, as there few converter tools which properly convert Word's generated table.

Because we will end up making some changes to the document to fit within the eBook publishing guidelines, make a copy of the original Word Master document now. Copy the CreateSpace Master document and name it something like 'eBook Master date-of-edit'. Put the CreateSpace original someplace safe. From now on we'll work only on the eBook Master. We'll modify this document and use it to create both Smashwords and Kindle source documents. I normally end up with three copies of my document, one named *'CreateSpace Master date-of-edit'*, one named *'Smashwords Master date-of-edit'*, and one named *'Kindle Master date-of-edit'*. I keep the date of edit in the file name so I can track documents if I need to make changes and re-upload at some point in the future. I also tend to create three folders for each book on my PC, named *'CreateSpace', 'Smashwords'* and *'Kindle',* so all files to do with each publication are stored together.

For backup and security purposes we will do the same as we did with our CreateSpace versions. Each time we edit the document we'll create a backup copy with the appropriate date in the file name. That way we can always back up a day or two, rather than having to recreate everything from scratch. We'll also store a copy of our backups on a separate physical device in case our computer fails.

EBooks are read on a computer screen of some sort, be it PC, Mac or Android tablet, Smartphone, laptop or eBook reader. Because of this, the pictures do not need to be the same high-quality, high definition 300 or 400 dpi resolution images we used for the paper printed version. EBook pictures, like web pages, are usually formatted for either 96 or 72 dpi. For eBooks, I will first drop the resolution down to 200 dpi in my Master document. If that still leaves the file too large for the converters to handle I will drop down to 96 dpi.

This can be done either within the graphics tool FastStone, or directly within Word. If I have only a few pictures I may use FastStone for this step, but normally I'll just use the Word Picture tool.

Open the eBook Master Word document and click on one of the images in your text to open the Word picture toolbar.

One of the options on the toolbar is 'Compress Pictures'. It's the box with arrows pointing in at the four corners. Click on that box to get the picture compression options.

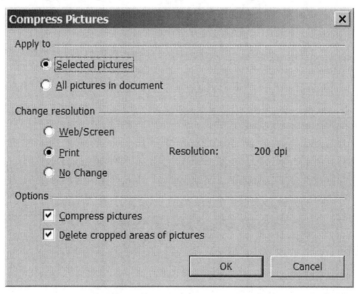

From here you can choose 'Selected pictures' or 'All pictures in document'. Select 'All pictures in document'. I leave the resolution setting at 'Print' which is 200 dpi, which is probably a little higher than needed, however it does reduce the overall file size significantly. If your book is very large, and compressing to 200 dpi still doesn't reduce the file size to something the publishing site will accept, repeat these steps and select 'Web/screen' which will reduce the resolution to 96 dpi, thus further reducing the size of the Word document.

For my 'how-to' book, **Shaping Stone**, compressing my pictures from 400 dpi to 96 dpi reduced my Word document size from two hundred and forty three megabytes down to a little over three megabytes. Reducing to 200 dpi still created a file more than ten megabytes in size, which is too large for the converters.

Next, go through the Word document and remove all page numbers, headers and footers, as none of these are useful items in an eBook. Many eBook reader devices treat the eBook contents as a single very long page. Screen breaks are controlled by font size and line spacing, which the reader can change at will, thus changing the 'page size'. This means that within an eBook reader (software or hardware) the number of pages in a book can vary dramatically depending on what the viewer has set as their preferred font size and line spacing. Page numbers thus become meaningless. Having headers and footers appearing on the reader screen would simply get very annoying, very quickly.

Page breaks and Section breaks are recognized by the eBook conversion tools, so breaks in the text which you placed to assist reading and story flow are retained.

Next, reduce any Titles which use very large font sizes. In a paper book, a 72 point main title looks impressive on a full page. On an eBook reader screen, it means you end up reading the title one or two letters at a time. The largest font you should use in an eBook is no more than 18 point. Some converters reject a file with fonts greater than 18 point. Some of the more esoteric fonts will be lost during the conversions, so be prepared to substitute fonts if required. Do a test conversion and review the results to see which fonts are lost.

If you haven't done so already, you need to create a 'thumbnail' version of the books front cover, at the recommended size of 2500 pixels by 1950 pixels at 200 dpi. Simply make a copy of your full sized book cover and re-size it to the required dimensions using the FastStone tool. EBook vendors use this thumbnail image on their web sites, so your original cover image will be too large for putting on a web. Smashwords also passes this smaller image to it's associated resellers, and it's important that all sites selling your eBook use the same eBook cover image.

If you are providing Internet links inside your document it is well worth converting those links to Word hyperlinks. In a paper book, any such links must be retyped to enter them into a PC browser. EBooks can link directly.

Highlight the link in your document and use Word's 'Insert, Hyperlink, Existing File or Web Page' option. This will embed the browser links inside your Word document, thus making it easy for your eBook readers to connect to your web based links. Most reader devices and software will allow the reader to click on the embedded link to open a separate browser window to that web site, directly from inside your book.

If you are using a table of contents, we have to do a little bit of manual work to help the eBook conversion tools build a Table of Contents that can be used by the e-readers. This is done using Word's 'Bookmarks' feature. If you have no plans to produce an eBook with a Table of Contents you can skip the next few paragraphs on Bookmarks.

First, re-create the Table of Contents in your document using Word's tool, but this time don't generate page numbers. Page numbers have real meaning in the paper version, but have no meaning at all in eBooks.

The Table of Contents should be correct and final as you've already published it in the paper version, however, double check just to be sure. Now, highlight and copy the entire Table of Contents and then paste it back into the document using the 'Paste Special, Unformatted Text', option. Make sure your paste completely replaces the Word built Table of Contents. This creates a Table of Contents which is plain text only, with no hyperlinks or internal Word codes.

Next, go to Word's 'Insert, Bookmark' menu option, make sure 'hidden bookmarks' is ticked and then delete all bookmarks that may already exist. Word often creates a number of default bookmarks which can confuse the document converters when we go to publish, so we need to get rid of them all.

Now go through your entire document and make each chapter title a 'Bookmark' using Word's Bookmark tool. Highlight the chapter title, press CTRL C to copy the title. With the chapter title still highlighted, click 'Insert, Bookmark', then use CTRL V to paste the chapter title as the Bookmark name, and click Add.

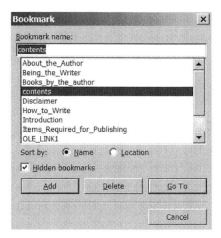

The name of a Bookmark cannot contain blank spaces so you will have to change any spaces to underlines before the Add button becomes functional. In the screen shot above, the Word default created bookmark named OLE_LINK1 should be deleted. All the other entries are bookmarks I created from my chapter titles.

Having Bookmarked each chapter title, go back to your Table of Contents and link each chapter title in the Table to the appropriate Bookmark. Highlight the chapter title in the Table, then click Word's 'Insert, Hyperlink, Place in this Document', option to open the linking screen.

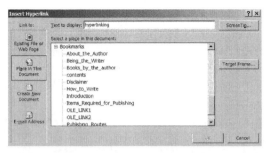

This option will display a list of all the Bookmarks you have created. Select the appropriate bookmark for your chapter link. The chapter title in the Table of Contents should be hyperlinked to the Bookmark of the same name. If you want you can also make the Table of Contents heading a Bookmark, and then link every chapter title in the book interior back to the Table of Contents Bookmark.

Once completed, you should be able to use Word's 'Go To, Bookmark' capability, and skip from the Table of Contents to a chapter heading and from a chapter heading back to the Table of Contents. While this may seem a little convoluted it allows the eBook converters to build a functional, hyperlinked Table of Contents into your eBook, making it available to the eBook reader menu bar. This provides your eBook readers with a complete, hyperlinked Table of Contents.

Lastly, go through your document and remove all tabs, all occurrences of more than three consecutive dots '...', all occurrences of more than two consecutive paragraph breaks '¶¶', and all tables. This can be done most easily with Word's 'find and replace' tool. However, it's best if you remember these constraints when writing and avoid them up front. Tables should be converted to lists.

When creating my original master document, I now incorporate most of these requirements into the CreateSpace master, with the exception of compressing the pictures and using tables. This means the CreateSpace Master will include the Bookmarks and Internet hyperlinks, even though they're of no use in the paper version. I also try not to use Tables at all, though sometimes it does make the paper version nicer to read.

I do this so the CreateSpace Master is truly the Master copy of my book. I can then make changes to the CreateSpace version, and republish the printed version. Then, to republish the eBook versions I simply reduce any large fonts (usually only on my title page), strip out the Headers and Footers, convert Tables (if any) and compress the pictures (if any). The biggest issue is that I have to rebuild the Bookmarked Table of Contents if there is one.

This avoids the potential problem of having to maintain and update multiple word documents if I later make changes to the content.

This process creates a Word document which can then be uploaded to both the Smashwords and Amazon KDP web sites for conversion and publishing as an eBook using their on-line tools. These tools will accept Word documents reasonably cleanly and will produce good quality eBooks. However, if you wish, you can use third party tools to create epub and mobi formatted files before uploading to the publishing tools. I don't do this as it adds in extra tools which you must learn and adds significant complexity to the process. If you wish to upload a pre-formatted epub (Smashwords) or mobi (KDP) file I suggest looking at tools such as Calibre and MobiCreator.

Technical Complexity: low to medium

Should have familiarity with Word cut and paste, inserting bookmarks and hyperlinks, find and replace using special characters, picture tool.

Creating a Smashwords eBook

Smashwords, to the best of my knowledge, was the first website to offer authors free publication of eBooks and free distribution to international book sellers. Being first was just the start, as they're now rated as the biggest as well. This quote is from their October 25th blog.

Bowker, the big US ISBN registrar, came out with research yesterday that named Smashwords the largest producer of eBooks for 2011. Pretty cool. They say we did over 40,000 titles last year (Smashwords authors and publishers actually released about 65,000 books through their platform last year, but who's counting.)

Also on October 25, 2012, this note:

This week Apple expanded the reach of the iBookstore to 18 new countries, bringing the total reach of the iBookstore to 50 countries.

Apple iBookstore Takes Smashwords to 18 New Countries

New Zealand | Brazil | Mexico | Argentina | Bolivia | Chile
Colombia | Costa Rica | Dominican Republic | Ecuador | El Salvador | Guatemala
Honduras | Nicaragua | Panama | Paraguay | Peru | Venezuela

Over 120,000 Smashwords eBooks now enjoy global distribution through the Apple iBookstore, these new stores included.

Smashwords also continues to develop relationships with existing and new distributors and resellers. For example, this was noted on the Smashwords Blog site, dated Oct 30, 2012.

Barnes and Noble launched their U.K. eBook store (www.nook.co.uk) yesterday, bringing with them over 114,000 Smashwords titles. B&N's move to the U.K. has been rumored for over a year, and publicly confirmed by B&N a few months ago.

In August of 2013, Smashwords added India's largest eBook reseller, Flipkart, as a new distributor and in September added Oyster.

Providing a free publication route and not charging anything until sales are made encapsulates the Smashwords paradigm in publishing. As can be seen by the actions of Amazon, CreateSpace and others, this paradigm is being emulated. It exemplifies a more positive and co-operative approach where neither party is required to outlay a large amount of money upfront.

As a leader in the eBook environment, Smashwords boasts over 50,000 authors, with over 169,000 titles published to date. In 2008, eBooks held less than 5% of the book market. By 2012, eBooks accounted for around 30% of the market. There are a number of reasons for this growing trend. The obvious one is the difficulty most authors have in gaining access to an agent, and thus to a publishing house. This entry barrier means a lot of authors simply don't or can't get into the traditional book market. The content of the market has been essentially controlled by the publishing houses, so a lot of content and authors simply never became available to readers.

With the advent of an organization like Smashwords, every author now has free and easy access to a multitude of markets. The only real requirement is to write a first class, high quality book.

The growing popularity of eBooks themselves is likely due to several factors. Reduced cost is key. A hardcover novel can cost $30 to $40. The same book as a paperback goes for $12 to $18. The same book as an eBook goes for $4 or $5, sometimes less. Economic theory says that as price decreases, volume sold tends to increase. Royalty rates also affect book price. An author under the traditional publishing house route would make a $1 or $2 royalty from a $20 sale. If the author can make that same $2 royalty from a $5 sale, it's more likely the sales volume and thus the authors total profit will increase, thus more authors will be prepared to sell at lower prices. Readers find eBooks more convenient, as they can carry fifty or more books around on their Smartphone and hundreds on their tablet. Selection is growing steadily, while content is expanding as more new authors, previously rejected by publishers who didn't accept their content or lack of sales record, are now entering the market. Subjects covered in eBooks are outpacing the traditional book market content.

Lastly, the book readers themselves can now control how they read their book, by adjusting font type, size, color and line spacing to meet their own personal preferences. Given the growth curve of eBooks, if you're an author, you really do want to get into the eBook market, and get into as many book sites and onto as many book reader devices as possible. Smashwords provides that access, and like everything else we've covered here, it's at no cost to the author, other than your time.

As I mentioned in the beginning of this book, Smashwords was my first encounter with this new publishing paradigm, and I've been a proud and productive Smashwords author ever since.

While I will be walking you through the process, much more detail is provided in the Smashwords publishing guidelines which can be downloaded at:

http://www.Smashwords.com/about/how_to_publish_on_S mashwords and

http://www.Smashwords.com/books/view/52

The Smashwords home page provides a number of other resources to the new author, including several presentations and analysis' of the Smashwords eBook markets. I recommend you review these resources as some of them may cause you to adjust your plan and / or pricing for your book.

Make a copy of the eBook Master file you created, and name it 'Smashwords Master date-of-edit'.

Start the publishing process by browsing to the Smashwords home site at http://www.Smashwords.com/ and create an account for yourself.

Once you've signed up you'll be presented with your 'dashboard'. The example below shows some of the books published to date under my account, provides links to the various control panels and shows the status and category of the books. All my books are in the Premium Catalog, which means I can authorize Smashwords to distribute them to the various third party international book seller sites. We'll get to channels and distribution management shortly.

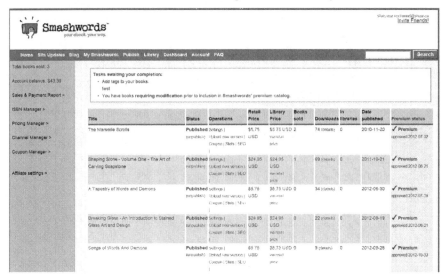

To start a new book select 'Publish' from the Smashwords menu bar. If you're working on a book already in progress, find the book on the dashboard list of titles and click on 'Upload a new version' or 'Settings', under the 'Operations' heading. You only use the 'Publish' option the very first time for each book.

The options along the left hand menu list will be discussed shortly.

Click on 'Publish' to begin the process of describing your book and uploading your document and cover for publishing.

Enter the title of your book. As we did with CreateSpace I recommend cutting and pasting the title from your book itself, as this ensures the book title is accurate. Open up your blurbs in Word and cut and paste both the 400 character and the 4,000 character blurbs into the appropriate fields. Smashwords uses both because some of its distribution partners use the short form and some the long form. Specify the language of the book and whether or not it contains adult content.

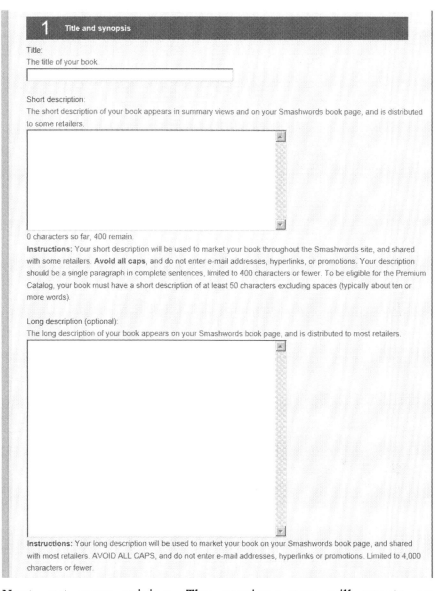

Next, set your pricing. The versions you will create on Smashwords will be distributed to multiple vendors and therefore will all have the same price. It's worth reviewing the Smashwords Blog for discussions on pricing and price points. Common prices for novels range from 2.99 to $6.99. Depending on your web browser and its settings, Smashwords will automatically display your shares of the various book royalties when you enter your cover price.

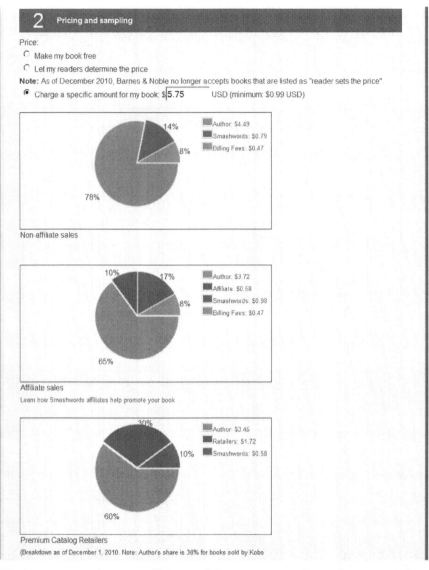

The next step is sampling and I recommend setting your free sampling to either 20% or 25% of your book. This allows readers to download the first part of your book for reading at no cost. If they are enthralled with your book they will come back and purchase the entire book.

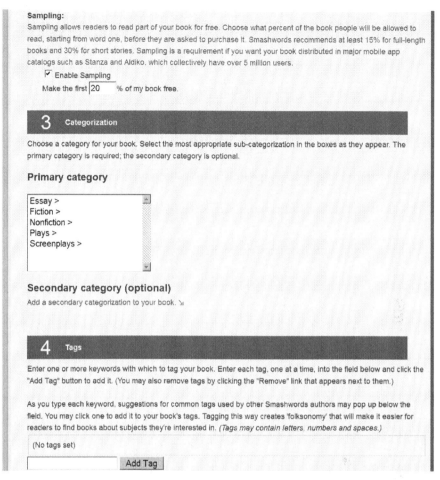

Assign a primary and secondary category to your book, finding those specific categories which best fit your book content.

In Smashwords, keywords are referred to as tags, and Smashwords allows you to add as many tags as you like. The tags will make it easier for readers to find your book based on keyword searches they're interested in.

Next we select the formats that we wish Smashwords to produce. This is where Smashwords shines, as it produces almost every eBook format you could want.

5   Ebook formats

Select the formats in which you'd like to make your book available. The more formats you allow, the more choice you allow your readers.

☑ epub
Your most important format. This is the format Smashwords distributes to the Apple iBookstore, Sony, Kobo, B&N, Stanza, Aldiko and others. Also very popular with Smashwords.com customers. EPUB is an open industry format.

☑ Sony Reader (LRF)
LRF is the format used on older Sony Reader ebook devices. The newer Sony Readers use EPUB.

☑ Kindle (.mobi)
This is one of the most popular formats for Smashwords.com customers. Mobipocket is an eBook format supported on the Kindle, as well as Windows PCs and many handheld devices. **DO NOT** disable this format.

☑ Palm Doc (PDB)
PalmDoc is a format primarily used on Palm Pilot devices, but readers are available for PalmOS, Symbian OS, Windows Mobile Pocket PC/Smartphone, desktop Windows, and Macintosh.

☑ PDF
Portable Document Format, or PDF, is a file format readable by most devices, including handheld e-readers, PDAs, and computers. A good format if your work contains fancy formatting, charts or images.

☑ RTF
Rich Text Format, or RTF, is a cross-platform document format supported by many word processors and devices. Usually pretty good at preserving original formatting from Word documents.

☑ Plain Text
Plain text is the most widely supported file format, working on nearly all readers and devices. It lacks formatting, but will work anywhere. For best results with plain text, your source document should not contain fancy formatting or images.

If there's a format you want that you don't see listed, please let us know!

The type of book you are writing will sometimes affect the formats you wish to create. For example a book with a lot of links in or with a lot of special formatting will not work very well in plain text. I normally produce my eBooks in the generic **.EPUB** format, the **.MOBI** format for Kindle, and Adobe's **.PDF** format. When I first started publishing I also created formats for the original Sony Reader (**.LRF**), the Palm Doc (**.PDB**), and the generic word processing rich text format (**.RTF**), but I have since stopped using these formats. The reason I stopped using them is because generic eBook readers (like Calibre) are available for all current hardware platforms and thus any hardware platform can now read either EPUB or MOBI formatted eBooks. PDF formats are also fairly universal but don't behave quite like an eBook.

Lastly we get to the file section. Click on the 'Browse' button to find your books cover image on your PC. This will be the smaller cover image file that you created for eBooks.

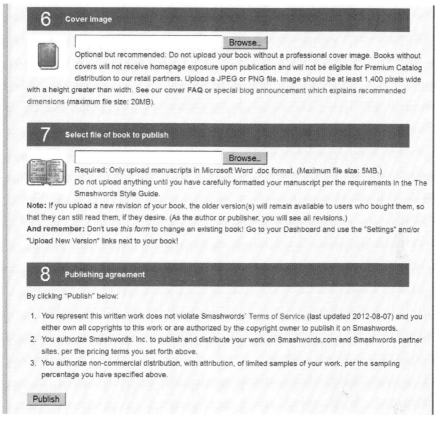

Click on the next 'Browse' button to select the book file to publish and select the file you created called *'Smashwords master date-of-edit'*.

Finally, read the Publishing agreement and if you agree click the 'Publish" button to begin the upload, conversion and publishing process. Your book will be added to the queue for conversion to the selected formats. The conversion process will also check for any possible errors in your document and send you an e-mail outlining anything which requires correction.

If corrections are needed, make them to your Smashwords master document and re-upload that to the Smashwords site.

Once you've uploaded at least one book on Smashwords you will automatically be taken to your Dashboard when you sign on. Make sure you upload newer versions from your Dashboard, not from the Publish page, as the Publish page is only used for the very first upload of a brand new book.

The Dashboard sidebar menu provides tools to control your books and the settings for the books, including an ISBN manager, a pricing manager and several other option managers. The ISBN manager allows you to set the ISBN for each book. Remember that each version you create requires it's own ISBN.

REMINDER: The ISBN you attach below CANNOT be the same ISBN you use for your print version or another ebook version.

Book	Author	Publisher	Published	ISBN	ISBN Source	ISBN Assigned	Actions
The Marseille Scrolls	Stephen C Norton (northwind)	N/A	2010-11-20	9780986755606	Self	2010-11-25	Edit ISBN Contact Info
test	Stephen C Norton (northwind)	N/A	2012-11-14	Non assigned			Assign An ISBN
Songs of Words And Demons	Stephen C Norton (northwind)	N/A	2012-09-28	9781927343289	Self	2012-09-28	Edit ISBN Contact Info
Shaping Stone - Volume One - The Art of Carving Soapstone	Stephen C Norton (northwind)	N/A	2011-10-21	9781927343005	Self	2011-10-21	Edit ISBN Contact Info
Breaking Glass - An Introduction to Stained Glass Art and Design	Stephen C Norton (northwind)	N/A	2012-08-19	9781927343098	Self	2012-08-19	Edit ISBN Contact Info
A Tapestry of Words and Demons	Stephen C Norton (northwind)	N/A	2012-06-30	9781927343227	Self	2012-06-30	Edit ISBN Contact Info

You cannot use the CreateSpace ISBN number for your Smashwords editions. Smashwords itself only requires a single ISBN per book, but as I showed on my example copyright page, your document should contain the ISBN numbers for all the formats you are producing. With Smashwords you have the option of using your own ISBN or using an ISBN supplied by Smashwords. I always supply my own .epub ISBN to Smashwords, as that is the format which will be distributed to third party sites.

The pricing manager allows you to set the price for each of your books. All prices are set in US dollars. You also have the option to set a different price for libraries if you so choose.

Smashwords maintains two categories of books. The Standard catalog is available from Smashwords only. The Premium catalog requires your book to meet specific publishing guidelines and content and is reviewed by Smashwords to ensure these guidelines are met. For example, to get onto the Premium catalog, your book must have an ISBN, meet epub standards and have a Smashwords Edition statement, as follows:

Smashwords Edition, License Notes
This book is licensed for your personal enjoyment only. Please do not copy or reproduce. Thank you for respecting the hard work of this author.

Once your book is accepted into the Premium catalog you then have the option of distributing it to most of the major international booksellers. As of September 2013 these booksellers include:

- **Sony Reader Store,**
- **Barnes & Noble,**
- **Kobo Books,**
- **Apple iTunes Books,**
- **Diesel eBook Store,**
- **Page Foundry,**
- **Baker Taylor's Blio,**

plus two library distribution outlets,
- **Library Director,** and
- **Baker Taylor's Axis360.**

Oyster and **Flipkart** (India) were added to the list in 2013. You can select whichever outlets you wish to distribute to. The channel manager also shows which books have shipped to the various distributors and which books are awaiting shipping. Smashwords continues to add distributors to it's list, so your markets are continually expanding.

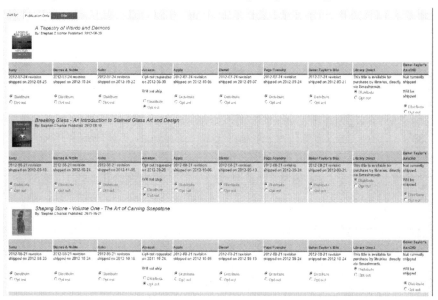

Note that Smashwords has an option to distribute their books to Amazon. When Smashwords first started publishing and distributing eBooks, Amazon did accept books from Smashwords. However, since Amazon implemented the KDP program, allowing Kindle books to be published directly by the author on Amazon, they have suspended the

Smashwords distribution link. For this reason I opt out of the Amazon distribution route on Smashwords and use the KDP route, which we cover in the next chapter. It does mean more work for the author, as you have to publish twice instead of once. Hopefully at some time in the future the Smashwords / Amazon relationship will be renewed. In the meantime, we can still publish on both sites at no cost.

Here's the summary status of your published titles:

Action required	No action required
☐ 1 book needs modification prior to resubmission.	✓ 5 books in Premium Catalog

Here's a summary of how many of your books are being distributed to each retailer.

Channel	Number of books				Next shipment to channel (approx.)	Notes
	Opted in	Opted out	Already shipped	To be (re) shipped		
Sony	6	0	5	0	Ships every Thursday or Friday.	Books appear approx 2 weeks after we ship
Barnes & Noble	6	0	5	0	Ships every Thursday or Friday.	Books usually appear within a few days of shipment.
Kobo	6	0	5	0	Ships daily.	Books usually appear within a few days of shipment.
Amazon	1	5	0	0	Ships every Thursday or Friday.	Ship date TBD. Smashwords and Amazon are working to complete technical integration.
Apple	6	0	5	0	Ships multiple times per day.	Apple manually reviews all books from all publishers and distributors. Their reviews usually take up to two weeks, sometimes longer.
Diesel	6	0	5	0	Ships every Thursday or Friday.	
Page Foundry	6	0	5	0		
Baker-Taylor's Blio	6	0	5	0	Ships every Thursday or Friday.	
Library Direct	6	0	N/A	N/A		
Baker-Taylor's Axis360	6	0	0	5		

Other tools on the dashboard sidebar menu include a 'Sales & Payment Report' which allows you to create downloadable reports on your book sales by channel, royalties due and payments made. Smashwords makes payments in US dollars a US bank account or to PayPal accounts on a quarterly basis, so you will need to set up a PayPal account for this purpose, if you don't already have one. All sales and payment reports are provided to you as Excel .csv files, available for download via the web page.

Smashwords also provides a tool to set up coupons for your books. For example, if you're doing a sales promotion or presentation where you've offered attendees a 15% discount off the cover price of your eBooks, you can generate a Coupon code and hand it out at the presentation. When attendees go to Smashwords to purchase your book, they enter the coupon code and get the price discount. Coupons can be set for individual books and coupons can be assigned validity start and end dates. Smashwords also does annual discount promotions to promote eBooks and readers, and if you opt in to those offers the coupons are generated automatically for the duration of the promotion. See the 'Notes from the Author' section for a coupon for this book if you purchased a paper copy.

Smashwords Coupon Code Manager

This page allows you to assign coupon codes to books which you can then share with prospective customers on your fan email lists, your blog or website, your social networks, or in your press releases and other promotions. Customers enter the code prior to completing their checkout to receive a discount.

Title	Base Price	Coupon Code	Coupon Price	Coupon Created	Coupon Starts	Coupon Expires	Actions
The Marseille Scrolls	$5.75	RAE25	$5.24 (~8% off)	2011-03-05			Canceled Reactivate
The Marseille Scrolls	$5.75	REW25	$5.24 (~8% off)	2012-03-07			Canceled Reactivate
Shaping Stone - Volume One - The Art of Carving Soapstone	$24.95	REW25	$18.71 (~25% off)	2012-03-07			Canceled Reactivate
A Tapestry of Words and Demons	$5.75						Generate Coupon
Breaking Glass - An Introduction to Stained Glass Art and Design	$24.95						Generate Coupon
Shaping Stone - Volume One - The Art of Carving Soapstone	$24.95						Generate Coupon
Songs of Words And Demons	$5.75						Generate Coupon
test	$10.00						Generate Coupon
The Marseille Scrolls	$5.75						Generate Coupon

You can also become an Affiliate which allows you to market other participating Smashwords books from your own website, blog, etc. and receive a percentage of their sales royalties. Other affiliates have the option of cross-marketing your book on their web sites.

From within the Dashboard, the upper left hand corner of the screen displays the number of books sold from Smashwords and the royalties due from all channels for this quarter. Note that royalties must exceed $10 in order to be paid. This contrasts strongly with the CreateSpace and Amazon minimums of $100 per currency before payment is made.

From the individual book line items on your dashboard you also have some other options. First is direct access to the 'Settings' for each book.

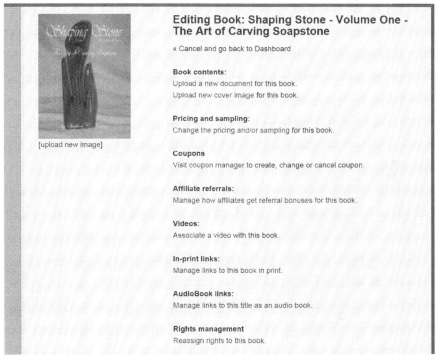

Editing Book: Shaping Stone - Volume One - The Art of Carving Soapstone

« Cancel and go back to Dashboard

[upload new image]

Book contents:
Upload a new document for this book.
Upload new cover image for this book.

Pricing and sampling:
Change the pricing and/or sampling for this book.

Coupons
Visit coupon manager to create, change or cancel coupon.

Affiliate referrals:
Manage how affiliates get referral bonuses for this book.

Videos:
Associate a video with this book.

In-print links:
Manage links to this book in print.

AudioBook links:
Manage links to this title as an audio book.

Rights management
Reassign rights to this book.

The settings page allows you to change any setting for the book, but also allows you to add information for the book, including such items as identifying multiple web locations for paper and audio copies of your book. You also have the option of uploading newer versions of both the book interior and cover, and updating descriptions, tags etc.

Next is the statistics panel for each book. This shows how many times your book page has been viewed on Smashwords, how many sample downloads and how many purchases have been made. These statistics are for sales direct from Smashwords only and do not show sales from the other distribution sites you've selected. Most of my sales actually occur on the third party sites, so I don't get too upset when my book stats show low downloads from Smashwords. More would be nice but it's not the end of the world.

30 days | 60 days | 90 days | Back to **The Marseille Scrolls**

Last 30 Days of Statistics for The Marseille Scrolls
Page Views

Visits to The Marseille Scrolls page at Smashwords.

Downloads (from paid customers)

Downloads of your full book, by customers, in any of the ebook formats it's available in. This chart is **NOT** an accurate indicator of the timing of your sales, since customers can purchase on one day and download multiple times on future days. See your Sales and Payments report for a full accounting of sales.
Since July 10, 2009

Sample Downloads

Downloads of the 20% sample version of your book in any of the ebook formats it's available in.
Since August 10, 2009

Lastly, and perhaps the most important, is the Search Engine Optimization panel, which allows you to see which search engines are finding your books and what the search returns look like. This gives you a view into the search engine environments, and thus you can update the engines with your links as and when you choose.

Search-engine optimization links for *The Marseille Scrolls*

This page provides links to search results on popular search engines that can give you a clue as to what parts of your book sample they've seen, and who out there might be linking to, or talking about, the book.

What have the search engines seen?

```
("The Marseille Scrolls" +site:smashwords.com)
```

- Google web search
- Yahoo! web search
- Microsoft Bing

What pages link to this book?

```
(link:smashwords.com/books/view/30704 OR
link:smashwords.com/reader/read/30704 OR
link:smashwords.com/extreader/read/30704)
```

- Google web search

General searches

```
("The Marseille Scrolls")
```

- Google web search
- Yahoo! web search
- Microsoft Bing
- Google blog search

```
("The Marseille Scrolls" AND "Stephen C Norton")
```

- Google web search
- Yahoo! web search
- Microsoft Bing
- Google blog search

« Back to Dashboard

For example, if your book is not appearing on Google, you can submit a web location to the Google search engine via the web link:

http://www.google.com/submityourcontent/

Most search engines provide the option to register your site on the search engine. Run a Google search for 'register my website with *searchenginename'* to find access points for the various engines. You can also register the CreateSpace and Kindle web locations for your books, but only Smashwords provides a tool to check your SEO returns.

As part of the interlinking capabilities on Smashwords, you can also share to your social media accounts, including Facebook, Twitter, Google+ and several others.

By now the Smashwords conversion process should have completed. Check your dashboard or your email for notifications of the success or the errors found which need correcting. Correct any errors and re-submit. If there are no errors you can then submit the book for inclusion in the Premium Catalogue, but before we do that let's just (guess what?) yes, let's check the converted files.

From your dashboard, click on the book title to go to the books sale page.

This is the page your readers will see if they purchase directly from Smashwords. Check the information displayed and make sure it's correct. Correct any errors or omissions via the 'Dashboard, Settings' pages. Scroll down to the bottom of the sales page to see the available formats.

Available ebook reading formats

You have purchased this book. **How to download ebooks to e-reading devices and apps.**

Format	Full Book
Online Reading (HTML, good for sampling in web browser)	View
Online Reading (JavaScript, experimental, buggy)	View
Kindle (.mobi for Kindle devices and Kindle apps)	Download
Epub (Apple iPad/iBooks, Nook, Sony Reader, Kobo, and most e-reading apps including Stanza, Aldiko, Adobe Digital Editions, others)	Download
PDF (good for reading on PC, or for home printing)	Download

Because you are the author you have full access to all formats. Download all the formats you selected to your PC or reader device. Fire up your reader software and read through each format, looking for anything that looks odd, inconsistent or is an error. Check page layouts. Does the poetry flow across the page the way you wanted? Do the embedded hyperlinks work and do they connect you to the correct web site? Do the fonts look right? Did the eBook Table of Contents come through properly. Adobe's Digital Editions reader shows the Table of Contents as a menu to the left of the book display. The Kindle Reader displays the Table as a page. How do the pictures look? See the next chapter for some detail views of the various reader displays.

As we've already checked the text multiple times I won't tell you to read the entire book text again, but definitely page through the entire book and check every page. Play with the reader controls, enlarge the text, change the font, see if anything 'breaks' your book. Check the book in multiple readers, and if you have multiple devices, use multiple readers on those devices. I check my eBooks on my PC, using MobiPocket, Kindle, Digital Editions and Calibre. On my android tablet I test with Asus MyLibrary, Sony Reader, Cool Reader, Google Play, Kindle, FBReader and Aldiko. They're all free downloads. Every now and again I'll check to see if a new reader has appeared and try that. Some readers are excellent, some leave a lot to be desired, but you need to check to see what your viewers are going to see when they buy your book. For example, Mobipocket Reader, viewing a KDP generated .mobi file will not show the Table of Contents. When viewing the Smashwords generated Kindle .mobi file, the Table of Contents is available and works well. Images will look excellent in one reader and may be almost illegible in another. Still, try and check as many as you reasonably can and correct any glaring issues if they are common across several readers. For eBook readers you may want to add a brief page to the purchaser suggesting a recommended reader software, or suggesting that if the display of your book is poor to try another reader and suggest one you know displays your book well.

Once you've finished checking your files and making sure they are acceptable, go back to your Smashwords dashboard. On the far right side is a column marked 'Premium Status'. If your book is acceptable there will be an option there to 'Submit'. Click on that to submit your book for inclusion in the Premium Catalog. The review takes a couple of days.

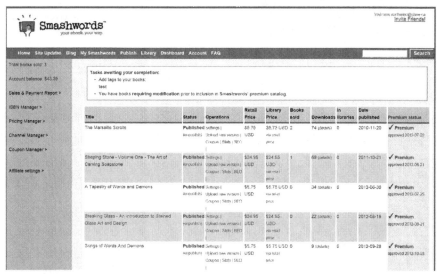

Once the book is accepted the status will show 'Premium' and the acceptance date. Premium status is required before you can distribute your book to the third party distributors, so it's <u>very</u> important you fix any issues in your book so it is accepted into the Premium Catalogue.

With the book in the Premium catalogue, you can designate which external distributors you want to use. I use them all! Why not? The more markets and sales sites your book is listed on, the more coverage you have and the more books you'll sell. It costs exactly the same amount to be listed on one distributor as it does to be listed on them all, and that cost is, well, obviously it's 'zero'.

Congratulations!

You're now finished. Your book is published in multiple formats and will appear on the external distributors sites you've selected under the distribution schedule shown on the Channel Manager page. Smashwords distributes to most vendors weekly, and then the vendor takes another week or so to post your book on their site, so your book should appear on the external sites within two to three weeks.

Now let's look at publishing on Amazon KDP for the Kindle.

Technical Complexity: low to medium

Filling out web forms, uploading files, installing software packages and using multiple eBook reader packages and multiple reader or tablet devices.

Creating a Kindle eBook

There are two ways to start building your eBook for a Kindle. The first is to simply select the option from your CreateSpace menu to publish on Kindle.

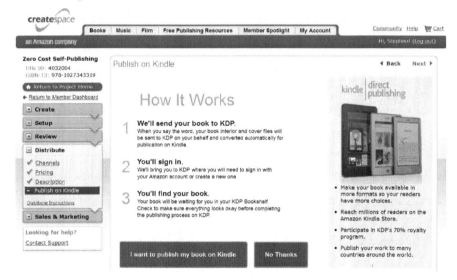

This option will send the book interior and cover files over to the Amazon publishing site and then transfer your login to the Amazon site. At this point if you don't already have an Amazon account you will need to create one, using the same email ID that you used for your CreateSpace account. If you used CreateSpace's Cover Creator and a CreateSpace cover style, rather than creating your own for cover for upload, you will need to use this route in order to get a copy of the front cover transferred over for use on the Kindle eBook.

The other way to begin building your Kindle book is to simply go directly to the Amazon Kindle Direct Publishing (KDP) site, create an account and begin building your book using your original files.

My preferred route is to do things directly using my own files. The CreateSpace option recommends using my original Word document rather than the PDF supplied to CreateSpace, so for me the two pathways are essentially identical, as I normally create my front cover from scratch.

Using your web browser, go to http://KDP.Amazon.com and create an account. Once you have created your account you are presented with a member dashboard which is very similar to the CreateSpace member dashboard.

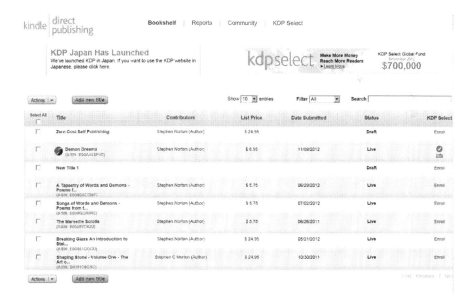

To begin a new title simply click the 'Add new title' button. To continue working on an existing project, double click on the book title. Either will bring you to the Title Setup Page.

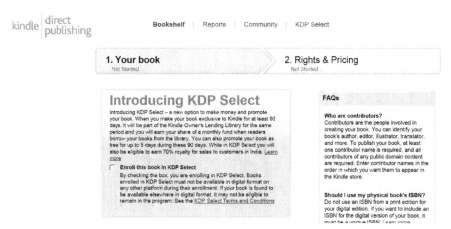

Ignore the KDP Select section for now, I'll come back to it later. Scroll down to begin entering the book information.

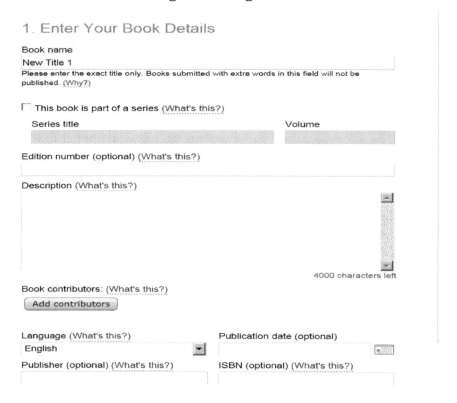

Enter the name of your book and any additional details, such as series name, edition number, etc. In the description, cut and paste your 4,000 character blurb into this field. As this is your account and your title you are automatically identified as the primary author. If there are any other contributors to the book you want registered, enter their names and contribution title under the book contributors fields.

Select the language the book is written in. Skip the Publication date as that will be completed automatically when you actually publish the book. Enter the Publishers name, which will be yourself or the name you wish to be published as. Enter the ISBN for the book. This cannot be the same ISBN as you used for the paper book you created for the CreateSpace version. As mentioned earlier, each format of the book must have a separate, unique ISBN. If you have your own, enter it. If not, leave the box blank. Note that unlike CreateSpace and Smashwords, KDP does not supply ISBN's for free. However, they will publish the eBook without an ISBN, which most other distributors will not.

2. Verify Your Publishing Rights

Publishing rights status: (What's this?)

○ This is a public domain work.

○ This is not a public domain work and I hold the necessary publishing rights.

3. Target Your Book to Customers

Categories (What's this?)

Add Categories

Search keywords (up to 7, optional): (What's this?)

7 keywords left

Select the appropriate Publishing Rights box, public domain or confirm you own the rights to the book and all its contents. As I've mentioned before, you must own all rights to all the content of your book, or have permission from the owner to use their content. From the drop-down menus, select the two most appropriate categories which best describe your book genre and then add up to seven keywords that could be used to find the book on a web search. The keywords will assist your readers to find your book based on search criteria.

If you transferred files from CreateSpace, your cover page should already be in place. If not, upload your book cover file by browsing to it's location on your computer and selecting it for upload. Remember to select the eBook sized image that you created from your paper book cover, the 2500 x 1500 200 dpi image, not the original full sized cover. The upload will take a few minutes so be patient.

4. Upload Your Book Cover

Upload image (optional)

No image available
Upload your image

Your book cover will be used for:

- the book cover inside your book
- the product image in Amazon search results
- the product image on your book's detail page

A good cover looks good as a full sized image, but also looks good as a thumbnail image. If you do not upload a cover image, a placeholder image will be used. See placeholder image example. You can change or upload a new cover image for your book at any time.

> Product Image Guidelines

    Browse for image...

Once complete you'll get a message, and a thumbnail of your cover will display.

4. Upload Your Book Cover

Upload image (optional)

Your book cover will be used for:

- the book cover inside your book
- the product image in Amazon search results
- the product image on your book's detail page

A good cover looks good as a full sized image, but also looks good as a thumbnail image. If you do not upload a cover image, a placeholder image will be used. See placeholder image example. You can change or upload a new cover image for your book at any time.

> Product Image Guidelines

Browse for image...

Next we upload the interior file for the book.

5. Upload Your Book File

Select a digital rights management (DRM) option: (What's this?)

○ Enable digital rights management

○ Do not enable digital rights management

Book content file:

Browse for book...

> Learn KDP content guidelines
> Help with formatting

Upload book

Select your Digital Rights Management option, either DRM protected or not. DRM prevents people from copying the eBook file after they have downloaded it, but it also introduces issues for readers who have legitimately purchased your book but now want to move it to another device. One train of thought is that DRM protects the author from pirating or illegal copying. A second train of thought states that the inconvenience introduced by DRM will reduce your readership due to the hassle. Not using DRM will allow your readers to easily manage your book, which will tend to promote it to readers. If you have several books published it's suggested that even though the first book may be 'pirated', a reader who enjoyed the first book is much more likely to purchase additional books from you. It is entirely up to you which option to choose. I assume my readers will purchase my books because they're enjoyable and useful, so I have chosen to <u>not</u> enable DRM.

Click in the 'Book content file' field, then click the 'Browse for book' button. Browse to where you have the eBook master Word document stored and select it for uploading. Alternatively, you can upload the Smashwords Master. Click on the 'Upload book' button. The upload will take several minutes so be patient. The KDP Word conversion is adequate, but I've found I get a better end product if I can upload a pre-formatted .mobi file, such as the one produced by the Smashwords process. There are also several third party tools which produce .mobi files, **Calibre** and **MobiCreator** being two such. You can also upload HTML files. Different uploaded source files produce slightly different .mobi eBook files so you may want to experiment a bit with your own book.

5. Upload Your Book File

Select a digital rights management (DRM) option: (What's this?)

    ○ Enable digital rights management

    ⦿ Do not enable digital rights management

Book content file:

[ ]	[Browse for book...]
› Learn KDP content guidelines › Help with formatting	[Upload book]

   ✓   Upload and conversion successful!

Once the upload is complete, download the Kindle preview file. You can use the on-line 'Preview Book' option but it's a rather basic HTML tool and doesn't allow for any viewer customization, so your book will display relatively poorly.

6. Preview Your Book

Previewing your book is an integral part of the publishing process and the best way to guarantee that your readers will have a good experience and see the book you want them to see. KDP offers two options to preview your book depending on your needs. Which should I use?

Online Previewer

For most users, the online previewer is the best and easiest way to preview your content. The online previewer allows you to preview most books as they will appear on Kindle, Kindle Fire, iPad, and iPhone. If your book is fixed layout (for more information on fixed layout, see the Kindle Publishing Guidelines), the online previewer will display your book as it will appear on Kindle Fire.

> Preview book

Downloadable Previewer

If you would like to preview your book on Kindle Touch or Kindle DX, you will want to use the downloadable previewer.

Instructions
> Download Book Preview File
> Download Previewer:
  Windows | Mac

I prefer to 'Download Book Preview File', which is a Kindle file, so I can review the book on my PC, laptop or tablet at my convenience, using my Kindle Reader software and other readers. This provides you with the same view of your book that your readers are going to see, so it's an excellent review method. The Kindle Reader software is available from the Amazon web site. Alternatively, I find the 'shareware by contribution' eBook manager and viewer Calibre is an excellent choice, as it will view eBooks in most of the formats available, including both .mobi and .epub formats. It will also create both .mobi and .epub files from Word .docx source files. The free MobiPocket reader is also an excellent tool for viewing Kindle format books, and is the companion to the MobiCreator tool.

The software packages mentioned above are all eBook readers for the PC. There are others available for both the Apple and Android hardware platforms. For Android there are Asus MyLibrary, Sony Reader, Cool Reader, Google Books (or Google Play), Kindle, FBReader, Aldiko Book, Kobo Reader, Nook Reader, Mantano Reader Lite, Bluefire Reader and others. For the Apple platform there are iBooks, Kindle, Nook, Stanza and others. Try the one that came pre-loaded on your device, and if that's not to your liking, find another one. The easiest way to find them is to simply do a search from your device. Install a few and try them out. Some are excellent, some not so much, however, there are enough available at no cost that you can find one that meets your requirements. I will note that from my experiences on Android, there are some which do an excellent job of text, photos and images, while others may do a great job on text but aren't so good with things like tables and images. I speak here specifically to the viewing of both the table and the screen shots, which I've used fairly heavily throughout this book. If your reader is not displaying the table as a table, or the screen shots so they're readable I suggest trying a different reader software. I've found that I use at least two readers on both the PC and my Android tablet, one for .mobi files and one for .epub files. I've yet to find a single package which does a good job on both formats, though Calibre comes closest. As mentioned earlier, small size images like screen shots will not display as cleanly as photographs and will not appear as readable, due to the limitations of the image size and dpi used on readers and eBook creation systems.

I've found that if the book is text only, you can upload your Word document directly into the Kindle converter. However if your document is larger than about twenty megabytes, or has a lot of images, I've found that doesn't always produce acceptable results and you need to use a different route. One alternate route is to complete your Word document and then perform a 'File, Save as', change the file type to 'Webpage, filtered' and then save your document. This will create an HTML file of your document along with a folder containing the images from your document. Copy both the html file and the image folder to a Windows 'zipped' folder and then upload the zipped folder to the Kindle converter as your document. This process automatically reduces the dpi of all images in the document down to no more than 96 dpi, and sometimes even lower. Another option is to create a .mobi file using one of the third party tools mentioned and upload that to the KDP converter. I've found this to be the most effective process.

For further detail on how to manage your document for Kindle you should download the latest version of the free Kindle book called 'Building your book for Kindle' from the Amazon KDP book site. You can read this book using either the Calibre reader or by downloading the Kindle reader in whichever format you need. Over the years the KDP .mobi creation process has changed substantially, moving from pre-building with MobiCreator and uploading a pre-built .mobi file, to uploading Word documents, either directly or via the HTML route described. Due to this changing environment it's best to review the latest edition of the Kindle building book, as provided by Amazon.

Once you have the downloaded Kindle file of your book, open it in a variety of readers and on a variety of hardware devices if available. Review the document, paying close attention to how it displays on the page. Is the indentation correct and what you intended it to be? Is the text layout as you intended? How do the pictures look. How do the tables look? The last two items are where you will want to use multiple readers. The native Kindle reader displays pictures as fairly small images, and there isn't any way to enlarge the image or zoom in on it. A few of the other readers do allow you to enlarge the image. Some readers do a better job of handling pictures than others.

Has the text converted over in a readable size? While all readers allow you to enlarge the text, some only have a few steps, small, medium, large, while others provide a much wider end user control.

As mentioned earlier, most eBook converters don't handle tabs well. For the poetry layouts displayed below I used Words 'Increase Indent' tool to arrange the lines of poetry the way I wanted them displayed. None of the converters had any trouble with the indent commands.

Some example Windows PC based Kindle reader displays are shown below.

Kindle Reader for PC

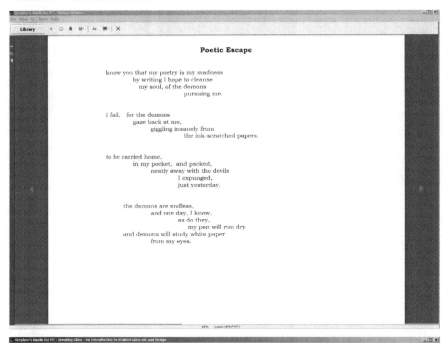

Poetic Escape

know you that my poetry is my madness
by writing I hope to cleanse
my soul, of the demons
pursuing me.

I fail, for the demons
gaze back at me,
giggling insanely from
the ink-scratched papers.

to be carried home,
in my pocket, and packed,
neatly away with the devils
I expunged,
just yesterday.

the demons are endless,
and one day, I know,
as do they,
my pen will run dry
and demons will study white paper
from my eyes.

Chapter 2 – Tools and Materials

Making stained glass objects is not highly demanding as far as tools go, but there are a few items that are must have's. In this section I'll give you a brief description of the tools used in stained glass work. In subsequent chapters, I'll get into the detail and techniques of how to use the tools as we create a lampshade from scratch.

Before anything else, you require a work space. A table or workbench is fine. I use a table about seven feet long and three feet wide, plus a few shelves on the wall above for storage of tools and glass. A few lights scattered around, both fixed and movable, help illuminate the work as I desire. As working with stained glass does produce some very fine chips and slivers of glass I recommend only working in a separate work area. A bench in the basement or garage is ideal. Cutting glass is not something you want to do on the kitchen table.

I painted the workbench white so make it as bright as possible, because working with glass requires good lighting. When cutting the glass I also add a sheet of white Bristol board. This gives the work surface a little bit of flex, making it easier to score the glass and easier to clean up.

There are some glass working tools you need to effectively do stained glass, and they will cost between $100 and $150 for the basics. Unlike some other crafts, the required tools are not likely to be found in the standard home workshop. There are not really substitutes you can 'get along with', and the lack of the required tool will make the task a lot less enjoyable, or in some cases, impossible. In brief, you need a glass cutter, pliers, grinder and soldering iron.

As stained glass requires cutting and assembling pieces of glass, you'll need a glass cutter. Various types exist, from a simple pencil cutter to a more advanced oil reservoir cutter, as shown below. This cutter allows a very small amount of oil to run along the back of the cutter blade, making it a little smoother to use. I use a standard light workshop oil, available from any hardware store, mixed with a little bit of WD40. I found the standard 3-in-1 oil I used on my bike was just a little

Calibre Reader for PC

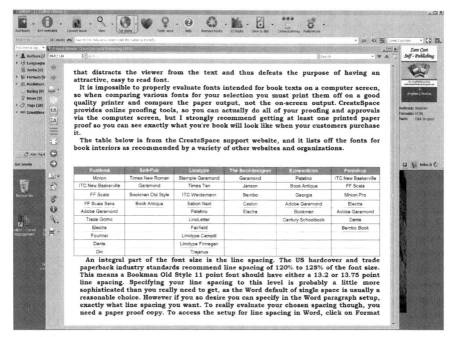

As we did repeatedly with the CreateSpace and Smashwords versions, review your Kindle version proof in detail, checking for all the same things as before. Multiple edit checks are key to producing a good quality book. The eBook version will display slightly differently in each of the software packages and differently yet again on the various eBook reader devices and tablets available on the market. The more packages and devices you can check your book on the better.

I own a Windows Vista PC, a Windows Win7 laptop and an Android ten inch tablet, so I check on those three devices. I use three or four packages on the PC and six or seven on the Android, playing with displays and options. This allows me to see what my readers will see, and thus make adjustments as and where I feel appropriate. I have tested on an Apple iPad 3 and the viewers in that environment appear to be very similar in capabilities and display to the Android apps.

MobiPocket Reader for PC

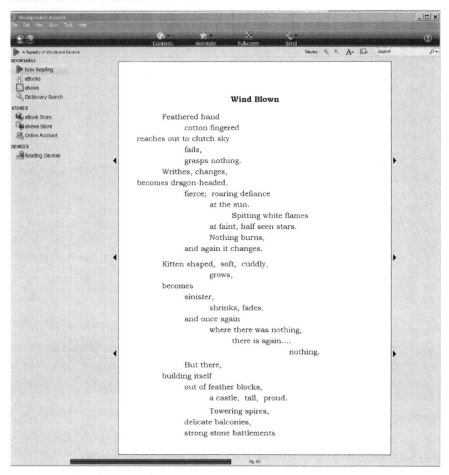

Notice that the readers have all done a good job of keeping the alignments of the text and images I set in my Word documents. Both MobiPocket and Kindle maintained the flowing layout I wanted for the poetry books. Calibre maintained the table as it looked in Word. Kindle has kept the photograph in the correct position, in-line with the text, though it has made it smaller than in the Word document and doesn't allow enlargement of the image. Some readers allow you to double click the image to drop into image mode, allowing enlargement, some do not. While most eBook reader tools give the viewer a wide range of options they can set, including font size and type, line spacing, and in some cases even background and font colors, the relative capabilities and trueness of display and layout are variable. The variation depends on hardware, display capability and reader software, so you will not be able to test everything.

The document has now been successfully uploaded to the Kindle converter, you've downloaded the Kindle file, re-done all the edit checks and everything looks good. Press the 'Save and Continue' button on the main Kindle Title page. This will take you on to the distribution and pricing page.

7. Verify Your Publishing Territories

Select the territories for which you hold rights: (What's this?)

Here you select your desired distribution territories, either world-wide or to specific countries of your choosing. I always use the 'Worldwide' option as it gives maximum sales coverage. If you chose 'Individual territories' you then have to go through a large list of countries (246 at last count) and select the ones you want to distribute to.

You next select the royalty level you wish to receive. For books under $9.99 you can chose either 35% or 70% royalties. To select 70% your book must meet certain criteria. Check requirements at the time you publish. For example, at time of writing, in order to select 70% royalty in India your book must be in the KDP Select program, which we'll discuss shortly.

8. Choose Your Royalty

Please select a royalty option for your book. (What's this?)

○ 35% Royalty

⦿ 70% Royalty

	List Price	Royalty Rate	Delivery Costs	Estimated Royalty
Amazon.com	$ 8.95 USD Must be between $2.99 and $9.99	35% (Why?)	n/a	$3.13
		70%	$0.21	$6.12
India (sold on Amazon.com) (What's this?)	☑ Set IN price automatically based on US price $8.95 🗨 ☒ Price must be between $1.77 and $7.12 to be eligible for 70% royalty for sales in India. You will earn 35% royalty at this price.Deselect "set automatically..." to input a new price.	35%	n/a	$3.13
Amazon.co.uk	☑ Set UK price automatically based on US price £5.59	70%	£0.14	£3.82
Amazon.de	☑ Set DE price automatically based on US price €6.97	70%	€0.16	€4.77

Amazon has more royalty areas for you to choose than CreateSpace did, but like CreateSpace you have the option of letting KDP calculate the price based on your US dollar cover price, or setting your own price for each area and currency. For some reason, Amazon KDP has set slightly different criteria on some areas, like India and Japan, with respect to a requirement to use the KDP Select offering. Amazon continues to add Amazon distribution sites, just as Smashwords continues to add third party sites.

8. Choose Your Royalty

Please select a royalty option for your book. (What's this?)

○ 35% Royalty

◉ 70% Royalty

	List Price	Royalty Rate	Delivery Costs	Estimated Royalty
Amazon.com	$ 8.95 USD Must be between $2.99 and $9.99	**35%** (Why?)	n/a	$3.13
		70%	$0.21	$6.12
India (sold on Amazon.com) (What's this?)	☐ Set IN price automatically based on US price $ 7.12 USD Must be between $0.87 and $200.00	**70%**	$0.16	$4.87
Amazon.co.uk	☑ Set UK price automatically based on US price £5.59	**70%**	£0.14	£3.82
Amazon.de	☑ Set DE price automatically based on US price €6.97	**70%**	€0.16	€4.77
Amazon.fr	☑ Set FR price automatically based on US price €6.97	**70%**	€0.16	€4.77

I normally select 70% royalties. For India I manually set the price to remain within the 70% guidelines. For more expensive books, like my 'how-to' books, the book price exceeds the allowed limit for 70% royalties, so they automatically default to 35%.

Lastly, select whether you wish to allow your buyers to share their copy of the book for the first 14 days after purchase under the 'Kindle Book Lending'. This allows a reader to buy your book, read it, and then loan that copy to a friend during the first 14 days.

9. Kindle Book Lending

 Allow lending for this book (Details)

By clicking Save and Publish below, I confirm that I have all rights necessary to make the content I am uploading available for marketing, distribution and sale in each territory I have indicated above, and that I am in compliance with the KDP Terms and Conditions.

<< Back to Your Bookshelf   Save and Publish   Save as Draft

As we're not using DRM, I see this as publicity. If a reader buys my book and then lends it to a friend, if they enjoy it, they're more likely to buy one of my other books. I believe that telling the purchaser that they can't treat my eBook the same way they would treat a paperback would simply be annoying and not accomplish anything, except probably drive them away from my books. I always allow lending.

Once you're finished setting prices, territories and lending, click on the tick box to confirm that you own all the rights covering the contents of the book, then click on 'Save and Publish'. This will publish the book to the Kindle bookstore.

Initiating publishing... this may take a moment

Your book is now being published. Please allow approximately 12 hours for English and 48 hours for other languages to be available for purchase in the Amazon Kindle Store. Until then, the book's status will be "In Review" on your Bookshelf

Go to my bookshelf

Just before we leave this section I do want to talk about the Amazon **KDP Select** Lending Library program, which was the first item we saw when we started a new title. This program allows you to put your book in the Kindle Lending Library, and Amazon will pay you a certain amount each time your book is borrowed from the Library. There are no sales royalties here because the book is only borrowed, however there is what basically amounts to a borrowing royalty. This seems to hover around $2-$3 per loan, but can change depending on how many books are enrolled in the library and how many loans happened each month.

The upside of this is that if your book is fairly expensive and sales are poor you might be able to make money by letting KDP Select loan it out. The downside is that to be eligible to be in the Library, you must have your eBook listed with Amazon <u>exclusively</u>. It cannot be distributed to any of the other on-line bookstores or appear in any other eBook formats. This means if you chose the Select program, you will not be able to use the Smashwords process and will not be able to list your book with other vendors such as Apple, Kobo and Barnes and Noble, etc. This limits your sales markets fairly severely.

How well the Lending Library will work for you, I believe, tends to depend on the type of book you have. For example, my 'how-to' books sell quite well in all formats and I have them on multiple distributors. Removing them from the other distributors and loaning them exclusively under the Amazon KDP Select program would probably reduce my sales income fairly significantly. By the same token, my poetry books have fairly low sales, as do most poetry books, so these might do better if I put them in the Lending Library. My sales on alternate distributor sites would go down, but if they're already low I might stand a better chance of making a higher profit from the lending payments. If you have several books published you might want to trial one book in Select to see what happens.

The Select Lending Library is free to the readers borrowing the books, so there is no cost barrier to borrowing a book by an author you know nothing about. This would seem to make it more likely someone will take a chance on a new, unknown author. I could potentially make my up for my lost royalties through the loan payments. Whether you use the lending library or not is entirely up to you. Just remember, if you use it you cannot use other distributors, which means you can't publish to Smashwords or distribute to Apple, Kobo, Barnes & Noble, etc. (This information is as of November 2012 and may change at any time.)

To enroll in the Select program, return to your Bookshelf and click on the 'Enroll' option in the KDP Select column of the title you wish to enroll. In the example, Demon Dreams has been enrolled in the KDP Select program.

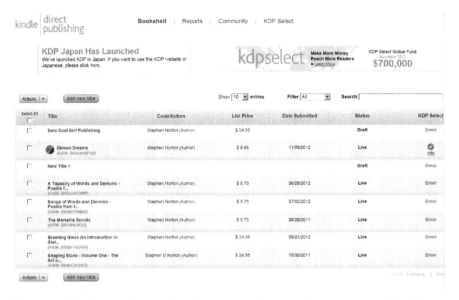

You will then be asked to confirm that your eBook is exclusively on Amazon and no other distributor.

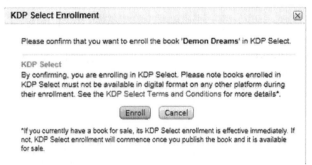

Amazon also provides the author with some publicity and tracking tools, the key ones being the author page and the author rank. We will get to these when we discuss marketing.

Congratulations, your book is now published on Amazon under the KDP program, and distributed to the world via the Amazon Kindle Book site.

Now you need to tell people about all your books and where to buy them.

Technical Complexity: low

Filling out web forms and installing software

Marketing and Publicity

Writing your book was the first major step on your journey. Publishing your book was the second major step. The third step was distribution and the forth is marketing. Marketing is the process by which you publicize your book and encourage readers to purchase what you've published.

Traditionally, say ten or fifteen years ago, your agent would sell your book to a publishing house and the publishing house would manage and run the publicity campaign. Normally a publishing house publicity campaign would last anywhere from ninety to one hundred and twenty days. Today, even if you can manage to get an agent and sell your book to a publishing house, unless you're already a major, well-known author with books on the bestsellers list, the publicity campaign is left entirely up to the author. Like everything else we've covered in this book, the publicity campaign can range in cost anywhere from nothing more than hard work on the author's part up to thousands of dollars. Hiring a publicity company or a publicity agent can run anywhere from $500 to $10,000 per month depending on their quality and how much work they do. Some of the vanity presses and self print companies that will print your document for you for a price, have also begun offering publicity and marketing packages in various shapes and sizes. Depending on what services you want these packages can run from anywhere from $500 to $3,000 per package.

If the publishing house's publicity campaign is successful in getting your books into the traditional brick-and-mortar bookstores, you can expect your book to survive on the shelves anywhere from thirty to ninety days. If sales are poor the book is likely to be taken off the shelf within the first thirty days. If sales are reasonable but not great you can expect to survive on the store shelf for maybe up to ninety days. Even a top-selling author can usually only expect their book to remain on the store shelf for a year.

It's become an interesting fact of the world that marketing and publicity of a book has now fallen almost entirely on the shoulders of the author. Most authors are not well positioned to run and manage publicity campaigns, but there are now some tools available to you that can be used. Happily, like the publishing and distribution routes we've used, these tools do not have the short shelf life of the traditional sales approach.

As a first step, the author should create his or her own personal webpage. This can be done reasonably simply and at minimal cost. Using myself as an example, I have created a webpage called www.StephenCNorton.com, using the Google webpage services. The name StephenCNorton.com is referred to as the domain name, and the domain name must be purchased and registered with a domain name management company via the Internet. Google provides both the webpage service and the Internet domain name for a grand total of $10 per year.

One book I read on marketing campaigns for authors recommended acquiring the domain name for your own name, all variations of your own name, and the titles of each of your books. When I first started publishing I took that advice and acquired the domain names 'The Marseille Scrolls.com', 'StephenCNorton.com', 'SCNorton.com', and 'NorthwindInk.com'. The domain 'StephenNorton.com' had already been taken by someone else. Each of these domains cost $10 per year and each of these domains have their own websites hosted by Google. I have since come to the conclusion that managing all those websites is more work than it's worth and have now dropped back to using only two, 'StephenCNorton.com' and 'NorthwindInk.com'. StephenCNorton carries all of my books, while NorthwindInk is the website I use for my publishing company. (Just like CreateSpace and KDP, I will do the technical work on your behalf for a fee.) All the other sites, while still being maintained at this point, will be phased out over the next few years. For now I have simply placed a link on the secondary sites pointing to my master site. Google provides some fairly easy-to-use web management and setup tools, so you don't need a great deal of technical know how in order to manage your own website.

This immediately highlights one of the major issues around an author running his or her own publicity campaign and marketing function. All of the publicity tools require both management and maintenance on a regular basis. For example StephenCNorton.com includes a list of all the books I have published and each book has its own page listing all of the sites where that book is available for purchase. Whenever I add a new book I must update the home page and create a new sub-page for the book details. My home page is shown below.

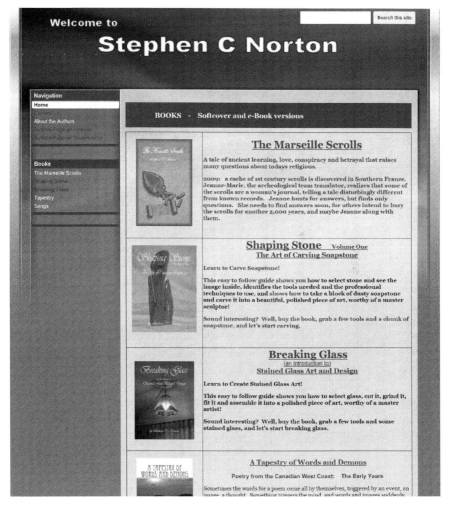

As I add a new edition or distribution site where each book is for sale, I must spend more time and effort updating the book page links. This is the web page specific to Shaping Stone.

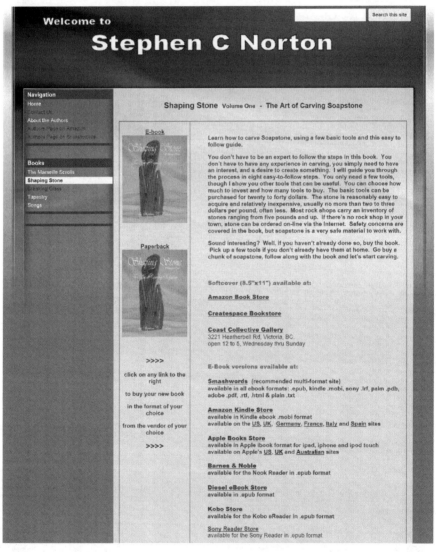

While not arduous in and of itself, updating each of the web pages takes time, time that I'd prefer to spend writing. I found very early on that I was spending almost as much time managing web pages as I was developing and writing my next book. Thus, while this may sound a bit strange, I lean towards <u>reducing</u> rather than expanding my use of publicity and marketing tools.

One excellent tool which is available, very useful from a marketing point of view and requires a minimum of upkeep is the 'Author Page'. Author pages are now available on both Amazon, and Smashwords. I'm hopeful that CreateSpace will make one available soon, but as an affiliate of Amazon they may chose to simply use the Amazon Author Page.

Amazon Author Page:

http://www.amazon.com/Stephen-C-Norton/e/B008MOY0IO

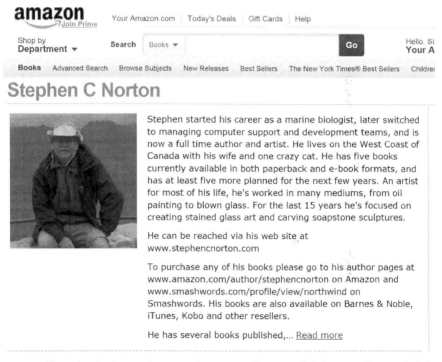

Immediately below the author profile and biography, which are created by the author, are listed all the books by the author which are available on Amazon. If you have both CreateSpace paper and KDP Kindle eBook formats available, they can both be listed. Amazon has a small quirk here. If you uploaded both versions on the same day, they will appear together. If you uploaded them days or weeks apart, they will appear as separate line items.

Books by Stephen C Norton

Showing 10 Results

Sort by New and Popular

All Formats Kindle Edition Paperback

Shaping Stone: The Art of Carving Soapstone by Stephen C Norton (Dec 3, 2011)

Formats	Price	New	Used
Paperback Order in the next 40 hours to get it by Monday, Nov 26. Eligible for FREE Super Saver Shipping.	~~$29.95~~ **$26.95**	$24.16	$42.36

The Marseille Scrolls by Stephen C Norton (Aug 11, 2011)

★★★★☆ (1 customer review)

Formats	Price	New	Used
Paperback Order in the next 40 hours to get it by Monday, Nov 26. Eligible for FREE Super Saver Shipping.	**$12.99**	$9.99	$29.14
Kindle Edition Auto-delivered wirelessly	**$5.75**		

Breaking Glass: Stained Glass Art and Design by Stephen C Norton (May 21, 2012)

Formats	Price	New	Used
Paperback Order in the next 40 hours to get it by Monday, Nov 26. Eligible for FREE Super Saver Shipping.	**$29.95**		

Demon Dreams: A Poetic Compilation by Stephen C Norton (Nov 6, 2012)

Formats	Price	New	Used
Paperback Order in the next 40 hours to get it by Monday, Nov 26. Eligible for FREE Super Saver Shipping.	**$16.95**		
Kindle Edition Auto-delivered wirelessly	**$0.00** *Prime* (read for free, Join Amazon Prime) $8.95 to buy		

Songs of Words and Demons: Poetry from the Canadian West Coast - The Middle years by Stephen C Norton (Jun 29, 2012)

Formats	Price	New	Used
Paperback Order in the next 40 hours to get it by Monday, Nov 26. Eligible for FREE Super Saver Shipping	**$12.95**		

A Tapestry of Words and Demons: Poetry from the Canadian West Coast - The Early Years by Stephen C Norton (Jun 29, 2012)

Formats	Price	New	Used
Paperback Order in the next 40 hours to get it by Monday, Nov 26. Eligible for FREE Super Saver Shipping.	**$12.95**		

Shaping Stone - Volume One - The Art of Carving Soapstone by Stephen C Norton (Oct 29, 2011)

Formats	Price	New	Used
Kindle Edition Auto-delivered wirelessly	**$24.95**		

Thus **Shaping Stone** has two separate entries, one paperback and one Kindle, while **The Marseille Scrolls** has both paperback and Kindle editions listed in a single entry. Both Smashwords and Amazon provide author pages that give you the ability to create a webpage on the sales site. Thus you can build or upload an author profile, biography and picture and present a single webpage which lists all of the books you have published on their site, with links to where they are available for purchase. The Amazon page is especially useful as it resides on Amazon and is actively promoted by Amazon, thus providing a well-publicized marketing tool directly on the Amazon site. The Smashwords page is just as useful as it allows you to publish other non-Smashwords sites where your book is available in print or as an audio book. It also allows you to publish a link to your own personal web site.

I have provided links from the sidebar on my personal page at www.StephenCNorton.com to both of my author pages.

Smashwords Author Profile

http://www.Smashwords.com/profile/view/northwind

Your Books

Songs of Words And Demons by Stephen C Norton
Price: $5.75 USD. 7090 words. Published on September 28, 2012. Fiction.
Sometimes the words for a poem come all by themselves, triggered by an event, an image, a thought. Something triggers the mind, and words and images suddenly, uncontrollably, flow. The image writes itself out and the demon puts down the pen, returning control to me. So, I give you the middle years of the demon scribbles: songs of words and images, thoughts, philosophies and visions.

Breaking Glass - An Introduction to Stained Glass Art and Design by Stephen C Norton
Price: $24.95 USD. 24680 words. Published on August 19, 2012. Nonfiction.
Learn to Create Stained Glass Art! This easy to follow guide shows you how to select glass, cut it, grind it, fit it and assemble it into a polished piece of art, worthy of a master artist! Sound interesting? Well, buy the book, grab a few tools and some stained glass, and let's start breaking glass.

A Tapestry of Words and Demons by Stephen C Norton
Price: $5.75 USD. 8250 words. Published on June 30, 2012. Fiction.
Sometimes the words for a poem come all by themselves, triggered by an event, an image, a thought. Something triggers the mind, and words and images suddenly, uncontrollably, flow. The image writes itself out and the demon puts down the pen, returning control to me. So, I give you the tapestry of poems from the early years of demon scribbles: words and images, thoughts and visions.

Shaping Stone - Volume One - The Art of Carving Soapstone by Stephen C Norton
Price: $24.95 USD. 21970 words. Published on October 21, 2011. Nonfiction.
Learn to Carve Soapstone! This easy to follow guide shows you how to select stone, see the image inside, the tools needed, the professional techniques to use, and how to take a block of dusty soapstone and carve it into a beautiful, polished piece of art, worthy of a master sculptor! Sound interesting? Well, buy the book, grab a few tools and a chunk of soapstone, and let's start carving.

The Marseille Scrolls by Stephen C Norton
Price: $5.75 USD. 83040 words. Published on November 20, 2010. Fiction.
2009: a cache of 1st century scrolls is discovered in Southern France. Jeanne-Marie, the archeological team translator, realizes that some of the scrolls are a woman's journal, telling a tale disturbingly different from known records. Jeanne hunts for answers, but finds only questions. She needs answers soon, for others intend to bury the scrolls for another 2000 years, and maybe Jeanne too.

The Author Pages are linked to all of your books which are available on that site, so if a reader finds one of your books, they can jump to the Author Page, and from there jump to any other book you've published on the site by simply clicking on the book title. This holds true for both Smashwords and Amazon Author Pages.

The other marketing tool available on both Amazon and Smashwords is the ability for potential readers to view the first part of your book. On Amazon this is the 'Look Inside' option, shown on the cover thumbnail image on the book sale page. This allows the potential buyer to view the first few pages of the book. The sample size is set by Amazon.

On Smashwords, you as the author can configure the percentage of the book you'll allow the potential buyer to download as a free sample. The Amazon approach allows the buyer to have a quick scan through the first few pages while on-line, but doesn't allow the author to adjust the percentage of the book made available, so they may not get much more than the front matter.

Smashwords requires the potential buyer to download a file, but gives the author the control to ensure the reader gets an adequate sample of the actual book contents. The sample size designated on Smashwords is carried over into the third party sales sites, so they can also offer samples to potential buyers. This is very important for new authors, as buyers are much more likely to spend money if they have had a chance to see some of what they're buying before paying for the book.

Available ebook reading formats

Single purchase gains access to all formats. **How to download ebooks to e-reading devices and apps.**

Format	Full Book	Sample First 20%
Online Reading (HTML, good for sampling in web browser)	Buy	View sample
Online Reading (JavaScript, experimental, buggy)	Buy	View sample
Kindle (.mobi for Kindle devices and Kindle apps)	Buy	Download sample
Epub (Apple iPad/iBooks, Nook, Sony Reader, Kobo, and most e-reading apps including Stanza, Aldiko, Adobe Digital Editions, others)	Buy	Download sample
PDF (good for reading on PC, or for home printing)	Buy	No sample available

Both these options allow the reader to pick the book up 'off the web shelf' and flick through the inside of the book, a virtual equivalent to browsing through the shelves of a bricks-and-mortar book store.

Other free tools which can be used as marketing tools are the social media systems which include Facebook, LinkedIn, YouTube, Twitter, Google+, etc. Again, while all these tools are available at no cost, you may find that managing and keeping them all up to date requires a lot more of your time than you are willing to spend. In my case I have restricted my use to Facebook and LinkedIn only. Facebook allows you to create a personal page, from which you link to friends, but it also provides you with the ability to set up specific pages for your books. Thus, from my personal page I also have Facebook pages about each of my books and my publishing company, with links out to their web sites. You then have the ability to invite your friends to 'Like' your book pages or send out event notices for events such as production of a new book or release of a new version. Facebook also allows you to create and circulate adverts on the Facebook pages, however this is a feature for which you must pay and as such I will do no more than mention it.

If you're one of those unusual authors who is also a very social person you can look into talking to your local radio or TV talk shows. Contacting your local newspaper book reviewer may result in a review published in your local paper. You may also have luck talking directly to your local bookstores and seeing if they will allow you to set up a table somewhere on their premises for a few hours to do a book release and author signing presentation. The option and cost to do any or all of these will be entirely dependent on your local companies.

Many of the books providing advice on marketing recommend adding reviews and comments from other authors to the back cover or in the front matter of your book. Previously that would have been a no cost item as you could simply send a copy of your book to a reviewer. However there are now so many authors out there that most reviewers have begun asking for a payment. For example one which I've seen mentioned several times in other books, provides a review service for authors. At the time of this writing the published standard service cost $425, while the express service was $575. I have to admit to some trepidation about the validity of a review for which the author must pay. Surely if I'm paying for the review I would expect to receive a good review, and if I can purchase a good review how 'real' is the review? Personally I've never made use of 'paid for' reviews but they are certainly available. Most also require a copy of the paper book and therefore you also have the cost of providing the book and paying for the shipping. While these are minor costs they can and do add up.

One possible route for acquiring 'real' reviews is through the distribution sites themselves. Amazon, Smashwords, Kobo, Apple, Barnes & Noble and most of the other distribution sites provide the ability for readers to submit comments about the book to the sales website. The author should monitor all these sites where his or her book is available for sale, scanning for the reader reviews, both to respond to the reader and to possibly use the comment as a review on their book. On my personal web site I have set up the ability for readers to send a comment to me and have received comments from readers as a result. You then have the option of asking the reader if you can use their comments in or on your book. In my opinion, these unsolicited reviews would be much more honest and independent of bias than a commercial review for which you have paid.

Other possible marketing tools include public events, book readings, speaking tours, and, depending on the content of your book, possibly even training or teaching sessions. One of the courses I took at my local college on how to prepare your book for delivery to a print company was given by an author. She'd written and self-printed a book, not surprisingly, on how to prepare your book for a print company. At the end of the course you were encouraged to purchase the lecturers book on your way out the door. All major credit cards were accepted.

If you write 'how-to' books, go talk to the managers of any local stores which are related to the 'how-to' subject. I have my book **'Shaping Stone, an introduction to carving soapstone'** in the local rock-hound shop. My other 'how-to' book **'Breaking Glass, an introduction to the Art & Design of Stained Glass'** is available in the local glass shop. Other possibilities may include museums if your book has an historical slant. As your book is locally produced and self-published, some of the local arts and crafts stores may be interested in carrying your book. The possibilities are endless, but they all require the authors energy and time.

Many marketing tools and techniques are available, but again the author must decide on which ones they wish to make use of and how much time and money they wish to dedicate to the marketing function. If you're one of the lucky ones on Facebook who already have five thousand friends, then Facebook would be an excellent marketing tool. If you're just starting your Facebook account and only have a few friends to begin with, then you should be prepared to expend a considerable amount of time while you build your friend base to a point where it's worth marketing to them. Some statistics suggest that one sale per thousand cold contacts is a reasonable expectation.

The intent of marketing is to get your name and the name of your book(s), out into the market place and recognized by the public. The more people who know your name, the more likely you are to sell your book. It's quite surprising how much more willing someone is to purchase your book if they have a chance to talk to you in person, or recognize your name from somewhere else. This can be done using the Internet social media tools like Facebook, but it can also be done using the more traditional routes as well.

Membership in a social organization gets your name out in front of people. However, these days most organizations require membership dues, so these are not 'zero-cost' options. As such, I'll make a few suggestions but not go into detail. Join your local Toastmasters International and give talks about your books or writing career. Research the many writers guilds and associations that exist and join those that seem appropriate. This will involve some work on reviewing and selecting the 'appropriate' associations though. A 'Google' search for *writers associations US* returned 70 million results in only 0.23 seconds. There are lots!!! of associations out there. Almost all of them require membership fees or fees for services of some type. Some even require a certain level of proof of professionalism, ie. you must have already sold a book to a major publisher in order to join, which can become a major 'catch-22' if you're a new author trying to break into the market.

Just remember, you don't have an unlimited budget, in either time or money. The more money you spend trying to publicize your book, the more you eat into the royalties you collect. The more time you spend managing and updating all the tools, memberships, speaking tours, etc, the less time you have available for writing that next great book. Try to find a balance. Personally, I've chosen the 'slow and steady' route. I make use of as many of the free tools as I feel I can devote the time to, without impacting on my writing time and energy too much. I leave the 'cost plus' and 'time plus' tools for later, for that time when my royalty income exceeds my regular salary. I've written a book on zero-cost publishing and yes, I do walk the talk. Even among the free tools, I look for tools which I can set up once and then leave for a month or two at a time, sites which do not require daily attention. Things like the Author Pages and my web site, where I only have to update them when a new book comes out, or a new distributor is added to the mix. I avoid things like Twitter and Blogs, because your followers expect daily (if not hourly) updates with a continuous stream of new and interesting information. If they don't get that they will lose interest in following your site and your blog or twitters will no longer do much as marketing tools. Budget your time just as frugally as you budget your money.

Another key issue with marketing and sales is to control your own expectations. Admittedly there are some authors who publish their book and immediately have it go viral. For every author like that there are probably several thousand who publish a book and sell nothing in the first year. Do not create such high expectations for your book sales that the reality can only disappoint you. On the flip side, don't be too disappointed if you only sell two copies the first year your book is available on the market. When I first entered the market with my novel, I sold exactly four copies in the first year across all my markets. I continued writing, adding books to my sites and adding sites where my books were available. In year two I sold twenty books, in year three I sold fifty. It seems that the longer you're on the market and the more books you have available for purchase the more sales you are likely to make. Unlike the traditional routes, where you had a ninety to one hundred and twenty day window to make yourself famous and sell millions of copes, the three environments we're using, CreateSpace, Smashwords and Amazon KDP, all provide you with an unlimited time on the market. A minor sales record will not result in your book being removed from the virtual bookshelves, and thus you have time to develop your market. I've found that the best marketing tool you can create is to write a second, third or forth book and get them all on the market. If you do have multiple books on the market, especially if they're a series around a common topic or character, try making one book free and use it as a 'hook' to bring readers to your books. If they like the free book, they'll come back and buy the second and third.

One thing I occasionally remind myself is that in Canada, copyright ownership of the book is good for seventy-five years after the author's death. It's similar in many other parts of the world. That means I can bequeath my book copyrights to my children, knowing that if I become incredibly famous after my death, as occasionally occurs with great artists and painters, at least my children or grandchildren will benefit from my work. My wife always smiles when I say that.

Writing should be an enjoyable thing to do. Once it becomes work, a daily grind, you tend to lose the enjoyment, especially if the grind isn't writing at all, but maintaining all the marketing and publicity tools. Enjoy your writing, enjoy setting up a few marketing tools that require a minimum of work and maintenance, then go back to enjoying the writing. Write a book, self publish it using the free tools I've introduced you to, then go back to writing another book. Occasionally you'll get a nice surprise in the mail when one of the sites sends you a cheque with your royalties. My last set of royalty payments bought me the tablet I now use to test eBooks on. Enjoy life.

Yet another thing to consider is the market to which you sell. I recently read a news article on the web which stated that there were 21.5 million tablets and 14.6 million laptops sold in the third quarter of 2012. In addition, 16 million iPhones were sold in that same quarter. IPhone competitors expect to sell equivalent numbers of their own Smartphones. Tablet manufactures expect to sell over 80 million units in 2013. Every one of these devices is capable of reading an eBook and sooner or later it's likely that every single one of those devices will carry at least one eBook and probably many more. For the new author the eBook markets are definitely the place to be. This tends to suggest Smashwords has an advantage in this market, as it produces multiple eBook formats, and not only makes them available in formats for all mobile devices, including both Apple and Android systems, but also distributes them to the sales sites that are delivering to these devices. The newer devices provide reader software and apps for both Android and Apple which are now capable of reading multiple formats, including both the generic .epub and the semi-proprietary Kindle .mobi formats. We're moving into an environment where proprietary formats are no longer an issue. In fact, most proprietary formats are being phased out as the generic .epub format continues to expand into the market.

At this point the majority of books published in North America are written and published in English. However there's nothing to stop us from translating our books into other languages and publishing them using the same free processes. The only issue is getting them translated accurately and properly. My recommendation is to find a human being if you're going to try translating your book.

As an experiment I translated a chapter of my first novel from English to French, using several different online and downloadable translator tools. Even my smattering of French could see that the result didn't quite look right. I then took the French translation and ran it backwards through the same translator, converting the French back into English. I did this with several different online translators. The end result in all cases was unintelligible, so I really cannot recommend that you use any of the computer-based translators to convert your book to another language. If you have a friend who is fluent in both English and another language then by all means try and convince them convert your book. Staying within the no cost environment that I'm promoting, maybe they would be interested in doing it for 50% of the royalties, or even 100% of the foreign-language royalties for one or two years. Given the number of smart phones that exist in Japan today, a Japanese translation would probably be very beneficial, but I have to admit I don't know of any free publishing site which produces Japanese language eBooks. Let me know if you find one and I'll add it this book.

The last statement highlights a major advantage of these forms of self publication: the ability to easily and quickly update the book as required. For example, suppose you realize after publication that there's a major error in the book, something which managed to get through all the proof-reading and editing, or conversely, some important new piece of information you'd like to add to your book. You can simply change it in your Master document, upload the new version to the various sites and the version containing the error or omission will very quickly disappear from the sales channels. The update isn't quite instantaneous, as your updated version will still have to go through the edit check and approval process on each of the publishing sites. There will also be some delay between accepting the updated version and replacing the updated version on the various sales sites. This would apply especially to Smashwords as their distributions to other sales sites take place weekly and then the other site takes one to two weeks to install the new version. Regardless, it does mean that you can correct and redistribute an updated version of your book relatively quickly and easily and completely cost free. If you've had significant sales of the erroneous book, some of the publishers will even assist you to notify those readers that a new, corrected edition is available. Worst case is you could put a 'comment' on the sales sites, informing readers of the update. Some sites will allow readers who have already purchased your book to download the updated version of the eBook again.

In the traditional method of the publishing house, your book would be produced in a mass print run of anywhere from five hundred to one thousand or more copies. If a major error was found after the print run was completed it was impossible to correct the print. A truly major error would require the destruction of the entire print run for that book and a reprint run, at either the publishers cost or, more likely, the author's cost. This issue also applies to the other method of self publication where the author would take his document to a printer and pay to have their book printed. The printer would provide the author with several boxes full of books, and if they were later found to contain a significant error, all those boxes would end up in the author's basement, of no value whatsoever as the error could make the book unsellable.

Using any of the three free publishing companies that I've outlined in this book, discovery of a major error would require no more than a couple of days work by the author, and a delay of no more than a month or so to correct. The next reader to purchase your book would receive an error free edition. There would be no direct cost to correcting the error. There would also be no boxes of unsellable books left to rot in the basement.

In the world of marketing, one item which I haven't yet touched on is direct advertising. This is a 'cost' item, so I'll only touch on it lightly. If you have a budget, you can generate public advertisements for your book. There are many local companies that provide sales fliers, newspaper inserts, envelopes full of coupons for selling all kinds of stuff. They come in your local newspaper and in your paper mail.

There are also on-line advertising systems. Google provides AdWords, in which you put ads on web search returns based on keywords you set. You can also set the amount of money you are prepared to pay for each advert and set a daily 'not-to-exceed' budget. They also provide tools for tracking how successful the ads are. Facebook will allow you to put up ads on their sidebars, and again you have options for the costs involved and the demographic you wish to place the ads with. All these options do cost money so you must decide how much you're willing to spend to sell your book. I did try AdWords for a while, early on in my career as a newly published writer, under a free-to-try program. People were viewing my ads, and some were clicking on them to go to my web site, but I didn't see any increase in sales of my book. Admittedly at that time I only had a single book for sale.

What I did find was that the cost of ads within the western world (US, UK, France, Australia, etc.) was <u>much</u> higher than ads within the less developed or non-western world. Within my defined budget guidelines, I think I was advertising to a market that had little interest in my novel. Advertising to the correct demographic would probably have been more effective, but would have cost significantly more money.

I have implemented sales banners on my car doors, bumper stickers and business cards, all relatively inexpensive forms of advertising. They're limited to my immediate geographic zone though. If you don't see my car, you don't see the advert. I do occasionally get asked for a business card from someone seeing the car door banner advertising my publishing company. I've never had someone ask me about the sales banner for my novel. Mostly I get interest in my books from word-of-mouth or from cold sales via the Internet book seller sites.

Advertising does work, but it does cost money. I fund my publishing career solely from my royalties, so I'm going to be on the slow path to fame and financial independence. I'm not prepared to risk any large amounts of money in promoting my books. Running major ad campaigns on AdWords and Facebook could easily eat up hundreds of dollars <u>per month</u>, if not more. I enjoy writing too much to want to put it on a 'must recover my investment' basis. Are you prepared to take more risk? That's entirely up to you. You've now successfully published your book at no cost, and have distributed it to the major retail web sites, covering the global market. The rest is entirely up to you.

Technical Complexity: low to medium

Filling out web forms, uploading files, installing software packages, creating and managing web sites and using multiple web based social media systems like Facebook and web based advertising systems like Adwords, if desired.

Revenue Streams, Taxes & Pricing

Using the three free publishing companies described in this book means you will get a number of separate revenue streams. CreateSpace pays royalties a month after the royalties have been earned, provided your account has more than $100 in it. This means your royalties from February will be paid in March. Amazon pays royalties when your account reaches $100. However, both CreateSpace and Amazon have a bit of a twist in their minimum payment thresholds. You have the ability to list your book with Amazon US, Amazon UK, and Amazon Europe. This means that you must reach 100 dollars or 100 pounds or 100 euros in sales before you will get a royalty check. The three streams run independently, so you can make $500 in US sales and get a royalty check, while your royalties in the UK and European markets will linger until they each individually reach 100 pounds or euros respectively. Your CreateSpace account pays royalties from CreateSpace only, but includes any CreateSpace paper copies sold via Amazon. Your Amazon account reports and pays royalties only for your Kindle sales through Amazon. This means a sale of a CreateSpace paper book, sold via Amazon, will appear only on your CreateSpace account, not on your Amazon account. If you're in the States you have the option of an electronic funds transfer into your bank account. If you're outside the States you get paid by cheque. Cheques are made out to the name you registered under and sent to the address you registered, so you must provide your real name and address.

Smashwords pays royalties on a quarterly basis, on any account exceeding $10, and pays into a PayPal account regardless of where you're located. If you have chosen multiple channels such as Apple and Barnes & Noble, your royalties from those channels will come from Smashwords, as Smashwords will collect and compile your royalties and send you a single payment. You do not deal directly with any of the other distribution and sales sites, nor do they pay you directly. All transactions are done through Smashwords. Use of the Smashwords payments reporting tool provides the detailed breakdown of how many books sold through which channels and what your percentage payments are from each channel.

As sales from your books are obviously considered to be income you should consult an accountant as to when and how you report this income on your annual tax return.

Sales from all three publishing systems are considered as US revenue streams, as they are all US based companies. As such, all three of the publishing companies are required to deduct 30% US taxes at the source. In order to recover the 30% taxes you will need to complete a US tax return.

However, if you are not a US citizen and do not reside in the States you may find that there are tax treaties in effect between the USA and your country which can reduce the amount of tax you have to pay. Some examples include:
Canada: 0%
Australia: 5%
U.K.: 0%
Japan: 0%
India: 15%
South Africa - 0%
Germany - 0%
In order to make use of these tax treaties you will need to contact the US tax department and request a US IRS-issued Tax Identification Number, referred to as an ITIN. This process is fairly involved, though not difficult. I did this through Smashwords as it was the first publisher I began dealing with. They describe the process quite clearly in their help pages and while it was easy to follow it took almost 8 months to complete. All three companies will follow the same procedure and all three companies must be notified of your ITIN once you have acquired it. You only need one ITIN. You can use any of the companies to complete the process. I won't go into detail, as the process may change over time. I recommend you review the help pages from whichever publisher you chose whenever you are ready to begin the

process. In general though, the process is as follows (this is the Smashwords process which I used).

To begin you must request a hand signed letter from the publisher, and this can only be requested after your royalties cross a certain threshold. This first step took 4 to 6 weeks. To avoid receiving any royalty payments and having taxes deducted while I was acquiring the ITIN I chose to defer all payments from Smashwords. This meant all my royalties simply sat in my Smashwords account for those 8 months. Next, you download the IRS W7 form, complete it and send it to the IRS (the help pages will provide the current address to use), along with the hand signed letter from your publisher and a certified copy of your passport. The IRS will then send you an ITIN. This step took a significant part of the 8 months.

You then download a W8-Ben form, complete it, showing your ITIN and send a copy to each of the publishers you have chosen to deal with. Each of the publishers then register your ITIN with their finance department and from then on will provide royalty payments deducting only the amount of taxes required under the tax treaty.

One of the requirements of the IRS to issue an ITIN is a certified copy of your passport. While any notary will make a certified copy of your passport for a fee, ranging from $50 to $100, in Canada at least you can take your passport down to the passport office and they will make a certified copy for you at no charge. This option takes about three weeks to complete and requires you to surrender your passport for the duration, so don't plan on traveling while you're getting the copy made.

While acquiring an ITIN is a long process and requires filling out a number of forms, I found it was worth pursuing as I had no desire to complete a US tax return every year to get my money back from the IRS. It's also free!

There are alternatives to simply selling through the three companies. The most obvious one is to sell your eBooks or your paper books from your own website. I do not do this because I think it's just too complicated and takes too much time to manage properly. However, there are website services that will provide not only a website but also access to credit card services, thus allowing you to accept credit cards for payment. Like almost everything else, there is a fee for providing credit card services and the credit card companies also take a percentage of sales.

Selling your eBooks this way should be relatively simple as you simply provide a download for the eBook upon payment. Selling paper versions will be more complex as first you must order the paper copies from CreateSpace. This will probably not be a worthwhile route as your costs and effort would climb significantly. You would have to purchase the book from CreateSpace, pay for the shipping from CreateSpace to your address, and then pay again to ship from your location to the person who ordered the book from your website. Shipping costs are likely to exceed any possible royalty you would make from the sale of your book using this method. You would also have to deal with receiving orders, shipping orders and confirming delivery and payment. I prefer to leave all those hassles to the publishers and distributors. Alternatively, you could accept the order from your own website, then purchase an authors copy from CreateSpace and have it shipped directly to the ordering location. While I don't know of anyone who does this, I do have several clients for whom I have published their Memoirs via CreateSpace, and they then shipped copies to their relatives around the world, directly from CreateSpace.

When considering what formats to produce, some statistics should be kept in mind. Paper books do sell, but as they cost more to produce they must be priced higher, and the paper based market is slowly shrinking. While production costs may be higher, your chosen retail sales price cannot exceed the general market value of your book. For example, paperbacks in the general market, including novels, romance novels, fiction, science fiction, etc. sell for approximately $12.99 to $14.99 in paperback format. If you price your fiction book higher than that it will simply not sell. 'How-to' books tend to be priced higher, but they almost always require color photographs of the process they are describing. The production cost of a full color book is significantly higher than the production cost of a black-and-white book. As the variable costs of book production come from the number of pages, it's better to produce an 8 x 10 color book with fewer pages than it is to produce a 6 x 9 color book. Again the price of your how-to book should not exceed the general market price of how-to books in that field.

Mark Coker, the owner of Smashwords, has done some interesting analysis on sales from the Smashwords site, based on eBook sales, relating sales volume to the number of words in a book, to the price point of the book and to the genre of the book. These are all available from the Smashwords help pages, and I would strongly recommend reviewing them when you're deciding on how to price your book. Based on Mark's research I reduced the price of my novel slightly so it would fall into one of the price breaks he'd identified as having stronger sales volumes, and found my sales increased somewhat.

Basic economics theory states that as price decreases sales volume will increase, but it becomes a matter of finding the right price point to maximize both sales and profit. A free book 'sells' much better than a $5 book, but has no revenue or profit, so you'll get no royalties.

Technical Complexity: low to high

Low for downloading and filling out tax forms and mailing them.

Medium to high if you choose to sell books directly from your own web site. This will also incur costs.

Royalties

Let's look at royalties from the three sites. Note that all discussions on royalty levels and rates are subject to change by the publishers, at any time, without notice. This information is what was publically available during the last quarter of 2013, but should be taken as examples only, and is in no way binding. This is going to get a bit messy because I'm going to throw a bunch of numbers around, but stay with me. All prices are US dollars.

CreateSpace Royalties
(paperback)

My book **The Marseille Scrolls** in 6" x 9" paperback format has a cover price of $12.99. The paper book has 242 pages.

Sold directly from CreateSpace, my royalty is $6.62 (51%)
Sold via Amazon Books US, my royalty is $4.04 (31%)
Sold via Amazon Books UK my royalty is £1.74
                    (£1 = $1.61, so 1.74*1.61=$2.80, or 21%)
Sold via Amazon Books Europe my royalty is €2.50
                    (€1 = $1.29, so 2.5*1.29=$3.22, or 25%)
Sold via the expanded distribution channel, my royalty is $1.44 (11%)
                    (note that you have to pay a fee to get the expanded channel)

The appearance of lower royalties from CreateSpace is a bit misleading, and is entirely due to the fact that actually producing and shipping the physical book is more expensive than delivering the same book in an electronic book format.

In this case, the cost of book production was $0.85 fixed cost for setup, plus $0.012 per page.
Cost of printing one copy = .85+(.012*242) = $3.75

which comes off of the cover price of $12.99 before any royalty calculations can take place. This means the revenue from the sale of my book was actually $9.24, making my CreateSpace direct royalty 71% rather than 51%, and my Amazon US royalty 44%, on-par with the royalty payments from the other publishing sites.

The other thing to note is that these calculations are based on CreateSpace's default pricing of UK and European books as a conversion of the US price you set at the exchange rate at the time of the sale. You also have the option of manually setting UK and Euro prices if you so desire.

Smashwords Royalties
(multiple eBook formats with multiple sales channels)
Smashwords royalties are a little more complicated because they have multiple channels, selling from multiple countries. Generally the royalty percentage varies from 38% to 60% of your cover price depending on sales channel and sales location.

My book **The Marseille Scrolls** had an eBook cover price of $6.99. (I later dropped it to $5.75 based on Mark's analysis.)

Sold directly from Smashwords.
Smashwords cut = $1.02
My royalty = $5.72. (81%)

Same book, same price, sold through Apple Australia
Book price = 6.99 AUD (Australian dollar)
Australian VAT tax = 0.64
Retailer cut to Apple = 1.90
Smashwords cut = 0.63
My royalty = 3.87 US (after conversion AUD to USD) (55%)

Same book sold through Apple US
Book price = 6.99 USD
Apple cut = 2.09
Smashwords cut = 0.69
My royalty = 4.21 (60%)

Same book sold through Kobo Canada
Book price = 6.74 (US price converted to Canadian dollar)
Kobo cut = 2.02
Smashwords cut = 0.67
My royalty = 4.12 (58%)

Amazon Kindle Royalties
Amazon KDP (eBook) offers a choice of either a 70% royalty or a 35% royalty option. The 70% royalty rate is restricted to certain price ranges and available for sales in only certain areas of the world, such as: Austria, Canada, France, Germany, United Kingdom and the United States. It is also somewhat restricted depending on whether your book is in the Select program or not. The 35% royalty rate is applied to sales in much of the rest of he world.

The 35% royalty is calculated as:
35% = Royalty Rate x List price = Royalty

While the 70% royalty is calculated as:
70% = Royalty Rate x (List Price-Delivery Costs) = Royalty
Delivery costs are charged out as follows:
      Amazon.com: US $0.15/MB
      Amazon India: US $0.12/MB
      Amazon.co.uk: UK £0.10/MB
      Amazon.de: €0,12/MB
      Amazon.fr: €0,12/MB
      Amazon.es: €0,12/MB
      Amazon.it: €0,12/MB

My book **The Marseille Scrolls** in Kindle eBook format has a cover price of $5.75. The eBook is 886 KB in size.

This means my 35% royalty would be:
0.35 * 5.75 = $2.01 (35%)

My 70% royalty, sold from Amazon US, would be:
0.70 * (5.75 - 0.15) = $3.92 (68%)

Now compare any of these royalty payments to the royalty an author could expect to see from the traditional publishing route, which varied anywhere from 5% to 15%, with only the best selling authors getting the high end of the scale. My royalty from the sale of **The Marseille Scrolls**, as a new author with no sales track record, would most likely have been 5%, or $0.65 per book, less my agents fee of 15%. I would have ended up receiving a royalty in the range of $0.55 per book. That's quite a bit less than any of the zero cost self-publishing options.

Book price = 6.99
My base 5% royalty = 0.65
My agents percentage = -0.10
My actual royalty payment = 0.55 per book.

As you can clearly see, the world of publishing is changing. These new sites aren't really doing anything for free, but instead of charging you up front as the vanity and self-printing routes do, or risking their money but offering you a much smaller royalty, as the traditional print publishing houses do, these new Internet based companies offer you a service up front at no charge, help you make sales from their sites at no charge, and then take their percentage off the top when you do make a sale. Yet they still pay you a higher royalty than the more traditional publishing routes. This is the new publishing paradigm. Easier for the new author to break into the market, a much bigger market for everyone to play in, and a risk sharing, cost sharing, profit sharing model which benefits all parties involved.

You just can't beat that.

Conclusions and Final Words

That concludes my guided tour through self publishing your book at zero cost. We have covered

- Being the writer and being the publisher
- The basic requirements for publishing a book and marketing it globally
- Costs of the various routes you can take to publishing
- Preparing and formatting the book's Master copy
- The need for backups of documents
- How to deal with photographs inside your book
- The options for creating the book covers
- Learning to work with the tools available from CreateSpace, Smashwords and Amazon KDP
- Publishing and proofing your book
- Selecting sales channels and setting book pricing
- Reviewing the marketing and publicity options and tools
- Discussed payment processes, taxes and tax treaties
- Reviewed the potential royalties

You should now be well positioned to go ahead and publish your book, if you weren't already doing that while you were reading this book.

I started publishing in 2009 and have been averaging one and sometimes two books published per year since then. The books I have published are available on all the book seller sites mentioned in this book. I have sold into the US, UK and European markets and have received royalty payments from all three of the publishers, Smashwords, CreateSpace and Amazon KDP. I can recommend all three publishers to you and be assured that you too can publish for free, make sales and receive royalties on those sales. There is no 'scam' involved here.

While all the companies discussed do offer additional services for a fee, their processes allow the author to do it all themselves at no cost if you are prepared to do the work.

I do have one comment on the offered services. CreateSpace and KDP both offer the services from their own internal resources. Smashwords recommends using external services and provides links to a community of people and groups who offer the various services. These 'third party' entrepreneurs are usually priced lower than the same services offered by KDP and CreateSpace. I have not used any of the 'services for a fee' offered by any of the three publishers myself, so I can offer no comments or recommendations. However, the services are available if you feel one or more steps of the process are beyond what you're prepared to do or comfortable doing. I myself offer the service of publishing a book on behalf of the author. Most of my clients are not that comfortable using computers for much more than email and browsing and feel managing the publication to be more complex than they wish to deal with. However, once the book is published, they take over management of the account and receive their royalties directly from the publishers.

Start with one book. Start with one publisher. As you gain experience, expand to the other publishers. Add a second book. Write more books. Publish more books. Make sales. Collect some royalties and repeat the process. All I ask of you is that you write the best damn book you possibly can, and edit and proof it as much as you can before publishing it. Your books and your reputation as a high quality writer are the best publicity you can create.

Thank you for buying and reading this book. I hope it has given you all the information you require to go ahead and publish your own book. As I promised at the beginning, if you're prepared to follow the steps and do the work yourself, you too can self publish your own books at zero cost.

Appendix

(in alphabetical order)

Zero-Cost Book Publishing Sites
Amazon KDP Publishing https://kdp.Amazon.com/
CreateSpace Publishing https://www.CreateSpace.com/
Smashwords Publishing http://www.Smashwords.com/

ISBN suppliers US and Canada
http://www.bowker.com (US)
http://www.collectionscanada.gc.ca/ciss-ssci/index-e.html

Graphics Management Tools
http://www.adobe.com/ (Adobe Photoshop or Elements)
http://www.corel.com/ (Paintshop Pro)
http://www.FastStone.org/ (FastStone Image Viewer)
http://gimp-win.sourceforge.net/ (Open Source Tool)

PDF Creation Tools
http://www.adobe.com/ (Adobe Acrobat Writer)
http://www.bullzip.com/ (Bullzip PDF Writer)
http://www.cutepdf.com/ (CutePDF Writer)
http://www.pdfill.com/ (PDFill PDF Writer)

EBook Reader and / or Creator Software
http://www.adobe.com/products/digital-editions.html
http://www.amazon.com/gp/kindle/pc/download
http://calibre-eBook.com/(multi-format eBook manager)
http://www.mobipocket.com/en/DownloadSoft/

Notes from the Author

Thank you for reading this book, I hope you enjoyed it, and hope you find it helpful in publishing your own books at zero cost. As a thank you for purchasing this paper book, you can also purchase the eBook version for **40% off** the eBook price. Just browse to https://www.smashwords.com/books/view/258154 to purchase and enter the coupon code HS72W. Offer good until Dec 31, 2014.

~~~~

For access to my other books, or to send comments, please contact me at my web site:

www.StephenCNorton.com
or
email: comment@stephencnorton.com

~~~~

This book was published by
Northwind Ink
Victoria BC
Canada

www.NorthwindInk.com

email: publish@northwindink.com

Northwind Ink is a small Canadian publishing house, specializing in small run editions while providing access to global sales via Amazon and other on-line distributers. We support new authors in most genres and those looking to publish their own memoirs. Our aim is to keep costs to the author as low as possible, while still producing a quality publication. We produce books both you and we can be proud of.

If you wish to have your book published by NorthwindInk send me an email.

Made in the USA
Charleston, SC
21 October 2016